CHILD'S WORLD

KING*f*ISHER

Project Editor Sue Grabham
Senior Contributing Editor Charlotte Evans
Assistant Editor Tara Benson
Section Editors Angela Holroyd,
Jill Thomas, John Paton

Senior Designer Janice English
Staff Designers Sandra Begnor, Siân Williams
Section Designer Ch'en Ling
Additional Design Smiljka Surla, Rachael Stone

Publishing Director Jim Miles

Art Director Paul Wilkinson

Additional Art Preparation
Matthew Gore, Andy Archer, Shaun Deal,
Julian Ewart, Narinder Sahotay, Andy Stanford,
Janet Woronkowicz

Picture Research Elaine Willis
Artwork Archivist Wendy Allison
Artwork Researcher Robert Perry

Activity Artist Caroline Jayne Church

Indexer Sue Lightfoot

Production Manager Linda Edmonds
Production Assistant Stephen Lang

Contributing Authors
Michael Benton, Michael Chinery, Fabienne
Fustec, Keith Lye, Christopher Maynard,
Nina Morgan, Steve Parker, Barbara Reseigh,
Dominique Rift, Jean-Pierre Verdet,
Florence and Pierre-Olivier Wessels,
Brian Williams

Specialist Consultants
Martyn Bramwell MA (Natural Sciences writer);
David Burnie BSc (Natural Sciences writer);
David Glover BSc, PhD (Science writer);
Ian Graham BSc, DipJ, FBIS, MCIJ
(Technology writer);
Professor B.W. Hodder BLit, MA, PhD
(School of Oriental and African Studies, University
of London);
Keith Lye BA, FRGS (Geography writer);
James Muirden BEd (Publications Consultant at
School of Education, University of Exeter and
astronomy writer);
Dr Elizabeth McCall Smith MB, ChB, MRCGP,
DRCOG (General Practitioner, Edinburgh);
Julia Stanton BA DipEd (Australasia consultant);
Dr David Unwin BSc PhD (Royal Society Research
Fellow, Bristol University)

Educational Consultants
Ellie Bowden (Curriculum Advisor for
Primary Science and Senior Teacher, Essex);
June Curtis (Primary School Teacher, Nottingham
and R.E. writer);
Kirsty Jack (Head Teacher, Primary
School, Edinburgh)

KINGFISHER
Kingfisher Publications Plc
New Penderel House, 283–288 High Holborn,
London WC1V 7HZ

First published by Kingfisher Publications Plc 1994
This edition published 1999
2 4 6 8 10 9 7 5 3 1
1TR(1BS) / 0699 / TWP / --(RNB) / 150AM

A CIP catalogue record for this book is available from the British Library

ISBN 0 7534 0439 7

Printed in Singapore

Contents

The Universe   5

Our Planet Earth   17

All Kinds of Animals   53

Plants   69

When Dinosaurs Lived   81

My Body   101

Science   131

Activities

Before you start each activity, collect everything you need and make sure there is a clear space. Wash your hands before cooking and wear gloves when touching soil. Wear an apron for gluing, cooking and using paints.
If an adult is needed, ask if they can help before you start.
Afterwards, make sure you clear up any mess and put everything away.

▷ Here are some of the materials that you might need for the activities. **Always** ask an adult before using anything that is not yours.

Recipe

500 g plain flour
150 g salt
1 mug water
food colouring

Make dough

Make dough for some of the modelling activities. Mix flour and salt in a bowl. If making coloured dough, add food colouring to water. Add as much water as needed to flour and salt, a little at a time. Stir. Turn out onto floured surface. Knead into a smooth dough. Make models. When finished, ask an adult to put them in the oven, on a low heat, for five hours. Paint the models when cool.

The Universe

What is the Universe?

The Universe is everything that exists. The Earth is part of the Universe. So are the Sun, the Moon and all the planets. Stars and clouds of gas and dust are also part of the Universe.

Scientists use telescopes and probes to learn about the Universe. We know a great deal, but there is still much that we do not know.

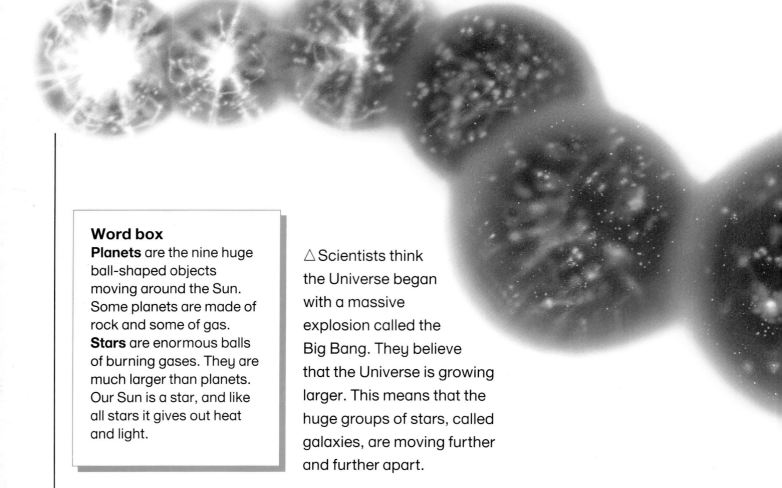

Word box
Planets are the nine huge ball-shaped objects moving around the Sun. Some planets are made of rock and some of gas.
Stars are enormous balls of burning gases. They are much larger than planets. Our Sun is a star, and like all stars it gives out heat and light.

△ Scientists think the Universe began with a massive explosion called the Big Bang. They believe that the Universe is growing larger. This means that the huge groups of stars, called galaxies, are moving further and further apart.

△ We can see stars, planets, galaxies, comets and clouds of dust and gas in the night sky by looking through a telescope.

Make your own Universe

Use a dark felt-tip pen to draw lots of small galaxies onto a balloon. Use the shape shown as a guide. The balloon is your Universe.

Watch the balloon in a mirror as you blow it up. You can see the galaxies moving further and further apart, just as scientists believe the galaxies in the Universe are moving apart.

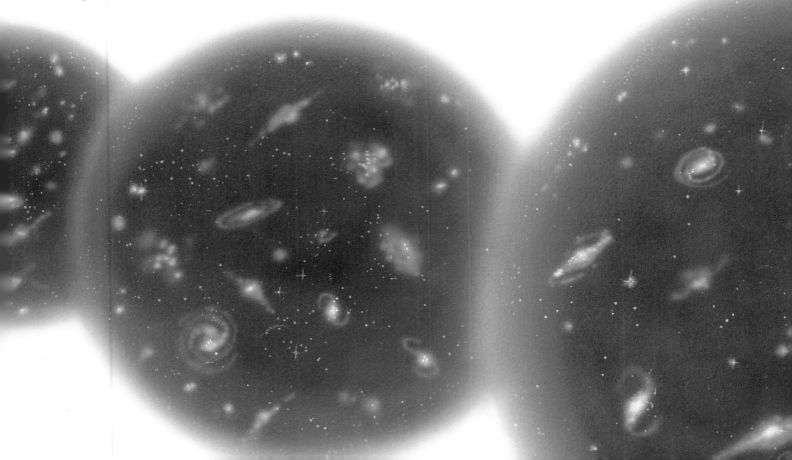

The Sun, our star

The Sun is a star. It is the closest star to us in the Universe. Like all stars, the Sun is a ball of hot, glowing gases.

Jets of gas, called prominences, often erupt from the Sun's surface. Dark patches, called sunspots, are very common. Sunspots are much cooler than the rest of the Sun's hot surface.

Never look directly at the Sun. Its light will damage your eyes.

core

prominence

▷The hottest part of the Sun is its core. The surface is called the photosphere.

▽ The largest prominences look like huge arches and may last for hours or days.

sunspot

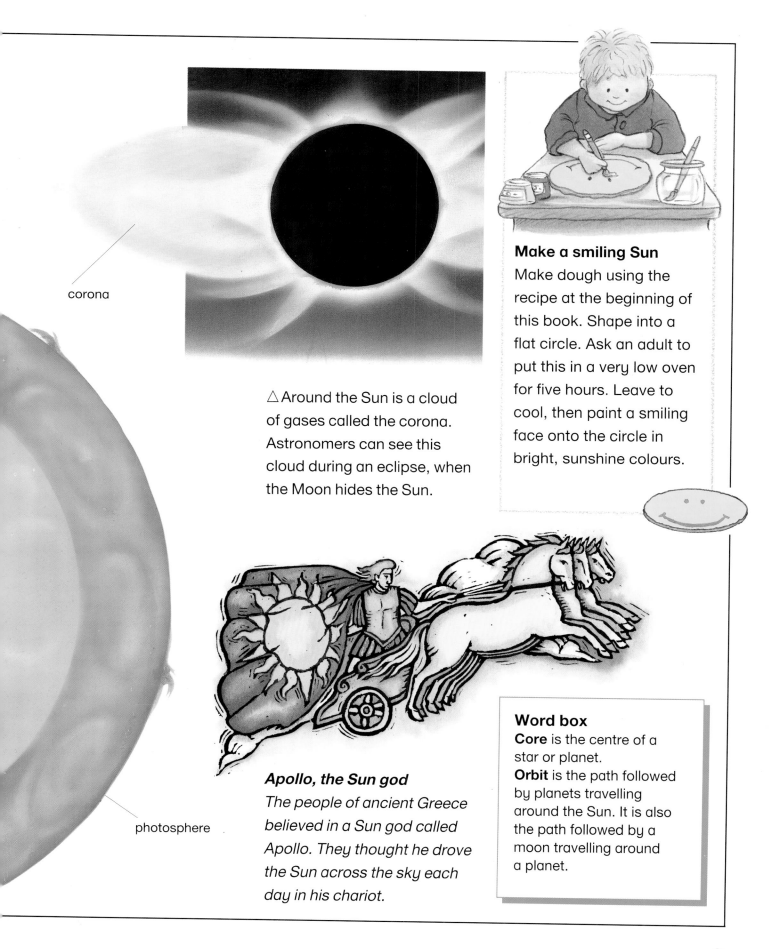

corona

photosphere

△ Around the Sun is a cloud of gases called the corona. Astronomers can see this cloud during an eclipse, when the Moon hides the Sun.

Make a smiling Sun
Make dough using the recipe at the beginning of this book. Shape into a flat circle. Ask an adult to put this in a very low oven for five hours. Leave to cool, then paint a smiling face onto the circle in bright, sunshine colours.

Apollo, the Sun god
The people of ancient Greece believed in a Sun god called Apollo. They thought he drove the Sun across the sky each day in his chariot.

Word box
Core is the centre of a star or planet.
Orbit is the path followed by planets travelling around the Sun. It is also the path followed by a moon travelling around a planet.

9

The Moon

The Moon is Earth's nearest neighbour in Space.

We can see the Moon in the sky because it reflects light from the Sun. The Moon seems to change shape. This is because as it orbits Earth, different parts of the side facing us are lit up by the Sun's light.

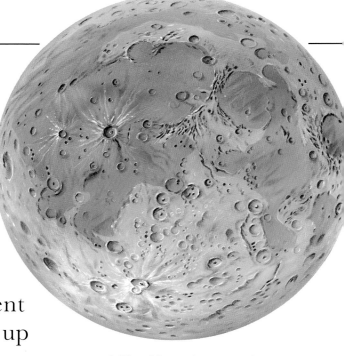

△ The Moon has no air or water. Nothing can live there.

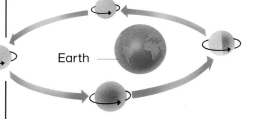

Earth

◁ Only one side of the Moon ever faces Earth, because the Moon spins on its axis in the same time it orbits Earth.

The king who wanted to walk on the Moon
(A Persian folk tale)

All the trees in the kingdom were used to make a box tower for the king to climb to the Moon. But still he needed one more. Foolishly, he asked his people to pass up the bottom box. When he fell to the ground, he wisely gave up the idea.

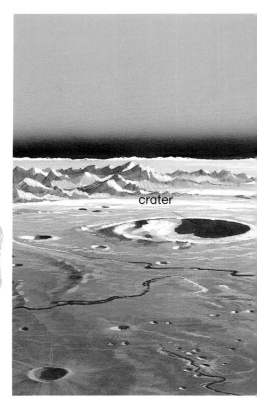

crater

△ The craters on the Moon were made when lumps of rock and iron, called meteoroids, crashed into the Moon's surface.

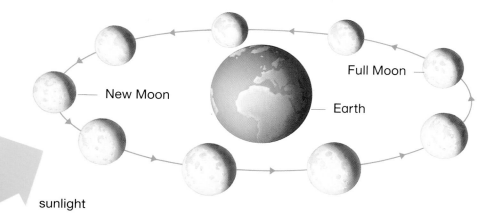

New Moon

Full Moon

Earth

sunlight

◁ When the Moon is between Earth and the Sun, the side facing us is so dark we cannot see it. This is a New Moon. At Full Moon, all of the facing side is sunlit so the Moon appears round.

▽ These changes are called the phases of the Moon.

Keep a Moon diary

To see the Moon's changing phases, record how the Moon looks each night for one month. Draw up a chart with the days of the week at the top and four rows underneath. Each night write down or draw what you see, even if it is cloudy and you cannot see the Moon.

Galaxies

On a clear night, you may be able to see a ribbon of white across the sky. This is the Milky Way. It is our galaxy, the huge group of stars that is our home in Space.

The Milky Way is just one of billions of galaxies in the Universe. Galaxies come in many shapes and sizes.

Sun

The man who met the Sun
(A Native American folk tale)

A man called Scarface and a chief's daughter wanted to marry each other. But first, Scarface had to prove to powerful Sun that he was worthy. He travelled to the sky in search of Sun. There he saved Sun's child. Sun was pleased and said that Scarface could now marry the chief's daughter. Scarface walked back down to Earth along the pathway called the Milky Way.

△ Spiral galaxies have two arms that slowly revolve round a central mass of stars.

△ This is what our galaxy, the Milky Way, would look like from far out in Space. It is a huge spiral of stars shaped like a pinwheel.

△ Certain galaxies are simply a great mass of stars. These are called elliptical galaxies.

Make a galaxy picture

On a large sheet of stiff, black paper draw a spiral galaxy in glue. Sprinkle glitter all over the glue. To reveal your galaxy picture, bend up the sides of the page and pour the spare glitter into a container.

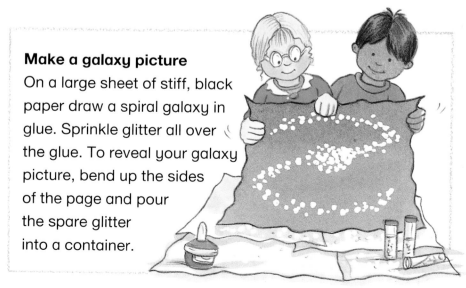

△ Some galaxies do not seem to have any shape at all. They are called irregular galaxies.

The Solar System

The Sun's family is called the Solar System. It includes all the planets, moons, comets and lumps of rock, dust and ice that orbit the Sun.

Planets are made up of rock, metal or gas. All the planets belong to the Solar System, but there are great differences between them.

▷There are nine planets in the Solar System. Jupiter is the largest. It is so large, all the other planets would fit inside it. Very little is known about Pluto, the smallest planet.

Uranus

Saturn

Mars

Jupiter

Sun

Mercury

Venus

Earth

◁These are the planets in the Solar System.

▷Most of the planets were named by astronomers after Greek and Roman gods. They chose a god to fit each planet's appearance.

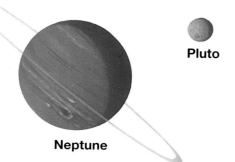

Pluto

Neptune

Mercury, the winged god

Venus, the goddess of love

Mars, the god of war

Jupiter, king of the gods

Saturn, father of Jupiter

Uranus, father of Saturn

Neptune, god of the sea

Pluto, god of the underworld

Sun

Mercury

Earth

Jupiter

Uranus

Venus

Mars

Saturn

Pluto

Neptune

Make a planetarium

Make the planets and the Sun from balls of plasticine of different colours and sizes. Use the main picture as a guide. Cut and paint card tubes to make stands.

Cover a table with paper. Place the Sun on a stand and put it in a corner of the table. Put the planets in their correct order from the Sun, as shown in the picture above.

Word box
Solar System is the Sun and everything that orbits the Sun.
Comets are huge lumps of ice, gas and dust which orbit the Sun.
Moons are natural, rocky balls that orbit planets.

15

Space stations

Living in Space may seem impossible, but already Russian cosmonauts have lived in Space for months, aboard the Space station *Mir*. Scientists are now planning to build a base on the Moon.

Star Trek
In the film Star Trek, Captain Kirk and his crew live aboard the Starship Enterprise.

However, scientists are a long way from inventing spacecraft like this one.

▽ When cosmonauts live on *Mir*, spacecraft without a crew bring them supplies from Earth.

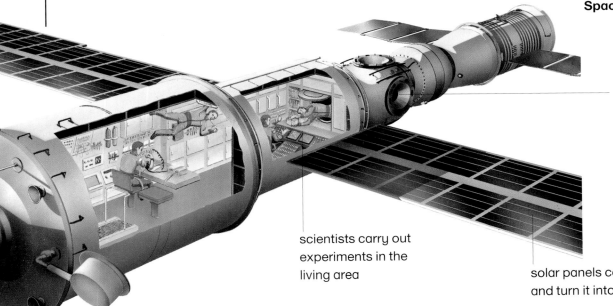

Space station *Mir*

docking port for visiting spacecraft

scientists carry out experiments in the living area

solar panels collect sunlight and turn it into electric power

▷ People could be living and working on the Moon one day. The first base will probably be a mining camp and may look like this.

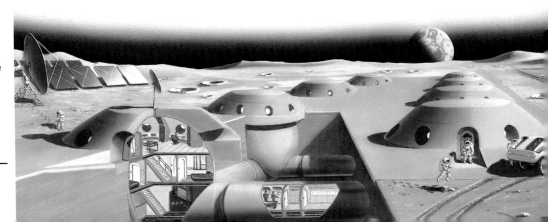

Our Planet Earth

What is Earth?

Our planet Earth is a huge rocky ball. It is one of the nine planets that travel around the Sun. From Space, Earth looks blue because seas and lakes cover nearly three-quarters of its surface.

Our planet has hot deserts, steamy rainforests and freezing cold North and South poles. In some parts, the land rises to make high mountains.

Can you find?

1 city
2 river
3 smoking volcano
4 elephant and her baby
5 rain cloud
6 forest

Earth, Sky and the gods
(A Polynesian folk tale)

At the beginning of time, Earth and Sky were joined together. The gods were trapped in the darkness between them and wanted to escape. They asked Forest to put his head on Earth, his feet on Sky, and push them apart. Sky fought back and started a storm, but Forest won. Earth and Sky were separated forever.

△ If you could see the Earth from Space, it would look like this. The swirling patterns are clouds. They are part of a thin layer of air around the Earth called the atmosphere.

Word box
Planets are the nine huge ball-shaped objects moving around the Sun. Some planets are made of rock and some of gas.
Atmosphere is the layer of air surrounding the Earth, protecting it from too much heat and cold.

Volcanoes and earthquakes

The Earth's crust, or surface, is divided into enormous pieces called plates. These plates are always moving very slowly. When plates move apart, the hot, runny rock below them rushes up to the surface and a volcano erupts. The hot, runny rock that comes out of a volcano is called lava. When plates bump or scrape against each other, earthquakes occur.

Erupt a volcano
Make a cone with thick card. Leave a hole at the top, as shown.
Put a shallow plastic pot in the hole. Place a little red powder paint and bicarbonate of soda into the pot.

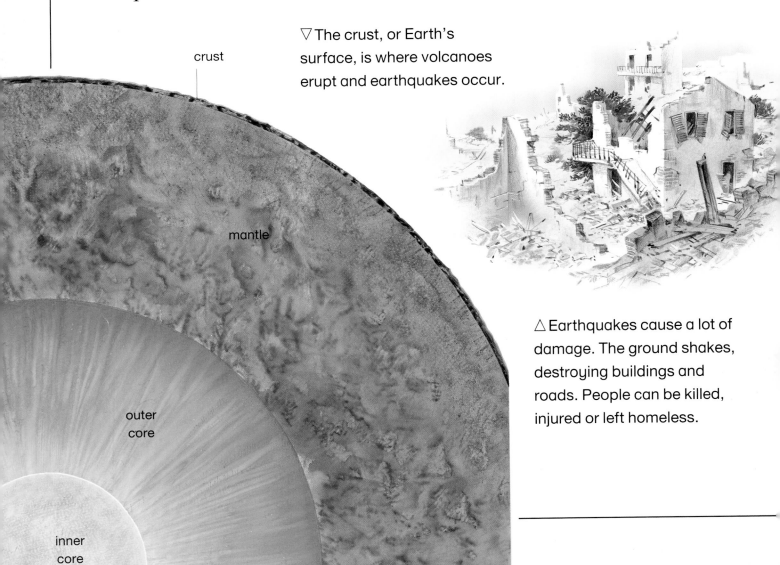

crust

▽ The crust, or Earth's surface, is where volcanoes erupt and earthquakes occur.

mantle

outer core

inner core

△ Earthquakes cause a lot of damage. The ground shakes, destroying buildings and roads. People can be killed, injured or left homeless.

Carefully add vinegar to make the volcano erupt.

▷ When volcanoes erupt, melted rock, called lava, is thrown into the air.

lava

Mountains

It takes thousands of years for mountain ranges to form. Many mountains are made when two of the crust's plates press against each other. When this happens, the rocks at the edges of the plates are squeezed together and pushed up into huge folds. A mountain becomes colder towards its peak, or top. Some mountain peaks are so cold they are snow-capped all year round.

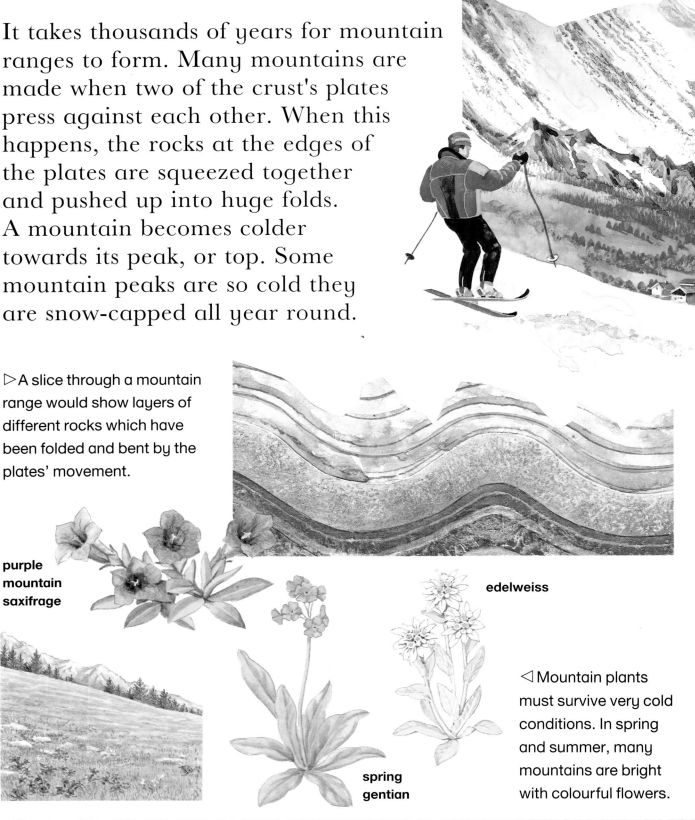

▷A slice through a mountain range would show layers of different rocks which have been folded and bent by the plates' movement.

purple mountain saxifrage

edelweiss

spring gentian

◁Mountain plants must survive very cold conditions. In spring and summer, many mountains are bright with colourful flowers.

△ Older mountains have rounded peaks because they have been eroded by the weather.

chamois

rocky mountain goat

△ In winter, chamois usually move down the mountain to the warmer forest areas. Rocky mountain goats have very thick coats so can survive nearer the top.

Heidi
(A story by Johanna Spyri)

Heidi moved to the mountains in Switzerland. She loved life in the mountains and the friends she met there.

Find the answers

Do older mountains have sharp or rounded peaks?

Are mountains colder at the top or the bottom?

The water cycle

The water cycle goes on all the time. It begins when heat from the sun turns water into an invisible gas in the air. This gas is called water vapour.

The water vapour rises, cools and turns into drops of water. These drops join together to make clouds. Wind blows the clouds over the land.

Water in the clouds falls as rain, snow or hail. It runs into rivers, which carry the water down to the sea, completing the cycle.

Word box
Water vapour is made of tiny drops of water held in the air.
Valleys are made when rivers wear away the land as they flow to the sea.
Glaciers are huge, slow moving rivers of ice.

winds blow clouds over the land

water vapour rises in the air to form clouds

seawater is heated by the sun and turned into water vapour

water falls as rain, snow or hail

Make rain in the bath
When you take a bath, water vapour rises as steam. When the vapour touches something cold, such as a mirror or window, it turns back into water again.

water runs into rivers and is carried back to the sea

What is air?

Air is a mixture of invisible gases. We cannot see it, taste it or smell it, but air is all around us. We can feel air when it moves. Moving air is called wind. Wind brings the weather, hot or cold, wet or dry.

All living things need air to breathe. So if there was no air, there would be no plants, animals or people on Earth.

Find the answers

What do we call the scale for measuring wind speeds?

What do dandelions use wind for?

▷Seabirds are masters at using the wind to glide and soar above the waves. Upward air currents next to cliffs help these seabirds reach their nests on high, rocky ledges.

Word box
Air is the mixture of gases surrounding the Earth. We all need it to live.
Hurricanes are violent storms with very high winds. Tornadoes are more violent, but smaller and shorter lasting.

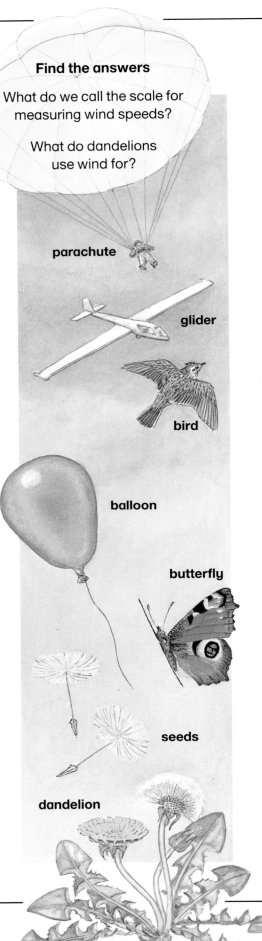

parachute

glider

bird

balloon

butterfly

seeds

dandelion

▷Animals, planes and gliders would not be able to fly without air. Plants such as dandelions use the wind to carry their seeds away. Balloons are filled with air.

▷There is a scale to measure wind speeds. It is called the Beaufort scale.

△Number 1 on the Beaufort scale is almost calm air.

△Number 4 is a breeze that shakes small branches.

Make a parachute
Securely fix four equal lengths of string to some plasticine. Cut out a square, about 40cm by 40cm, from a plastic bag. Use sticky tape to attach the string to each corner of the square. Hold the parachute high up and let it drop down.

△Number 7 is a gale strong enough to break branches.

△Number 10 is a strong gale. Buildings are often damaged.

The Wind and the Sun
(Based on a story by Aesop)

Wind and Sun had a competition to make a man remove his coat. Wind blew a fierce gale, but the man pulled his coat tightly around him.

Sun proved he was more powerful. He gently shone on the man, which made him take off his coat to cool down.

Storms and clouds

Storms bring clouds, rain, lightning and thunder. Lightning is a giant, hot spark of electricity that jumps between a storm cloud and the ground. Thunder is the noise caused by this spark. We hear thunder after lightning because sound travels more slowly than light.

cumulus clouds

▷Clouds are made from millions of tiny water droplets or ice crystals. There are many different kinds of clouds. The largest are thunder clouds, called cumulonimbus.

Thunder and Lightning
(A Nigerian folk tale)

Once Lightning, an angry ram, lived on Earth. Thunder was his mother. Lightning spat fire, burning down villagers' huts. Thunder followed him, shouting loudly at her son. The villagers pleaded with their king to send them away. He banished them to the sky. But you can still see Lightning's fiery rages and hear his mother, Thunder.

▽ Hurricanes and tornadoes cause damage. They rip up trees and buildings.

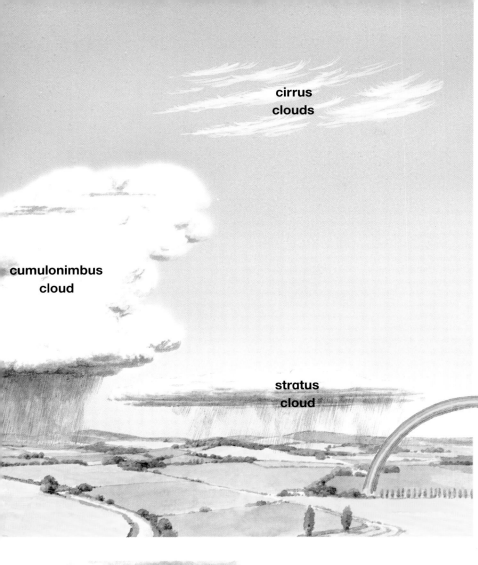

cirrus
clouds

cumulonimbus
cloud

stratus
cloud

△ Electricity builds up inside clouds and on the ground.

△ The electricity causes a brilliant flash of lightning.

Find the answers

Why do we hear thunder after we have seen lightning?

What are clouds made from?

△ Seconds later, there is a crash of thunder.

The seven continents

Spread out flat, the Earth looks like this map. The land is divided into seven continents. They are Africa, Antarctica, Asia, Australia, Europe, North America and South America.

Continents have different climates. Climate is the usual weather of a place. Can you find a hot, dry desert on this map?

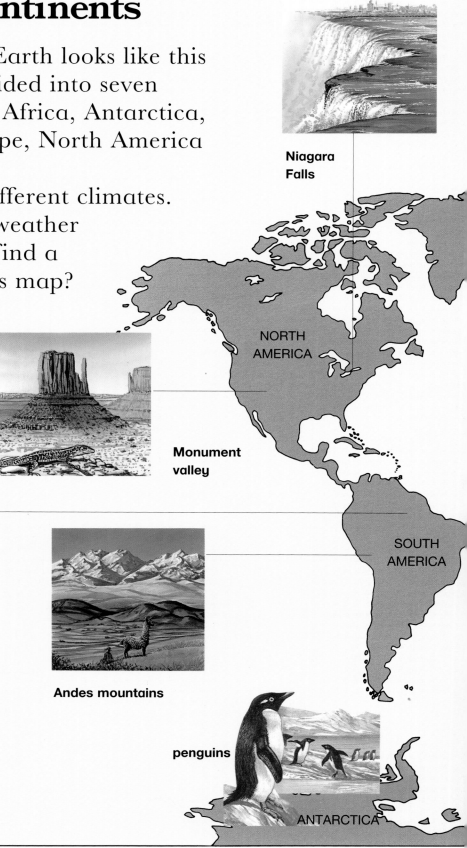

Niagara Falls

NORTH AMERICA

Monument valley

Amazon River and rainforest

Andes mountains

SOUTH AMERICA

penguins

ANTARCTICA

Word box
Continent is one of the seven largest areas of land on Earth.
Climate is the usual kind of weather found in a particular place.

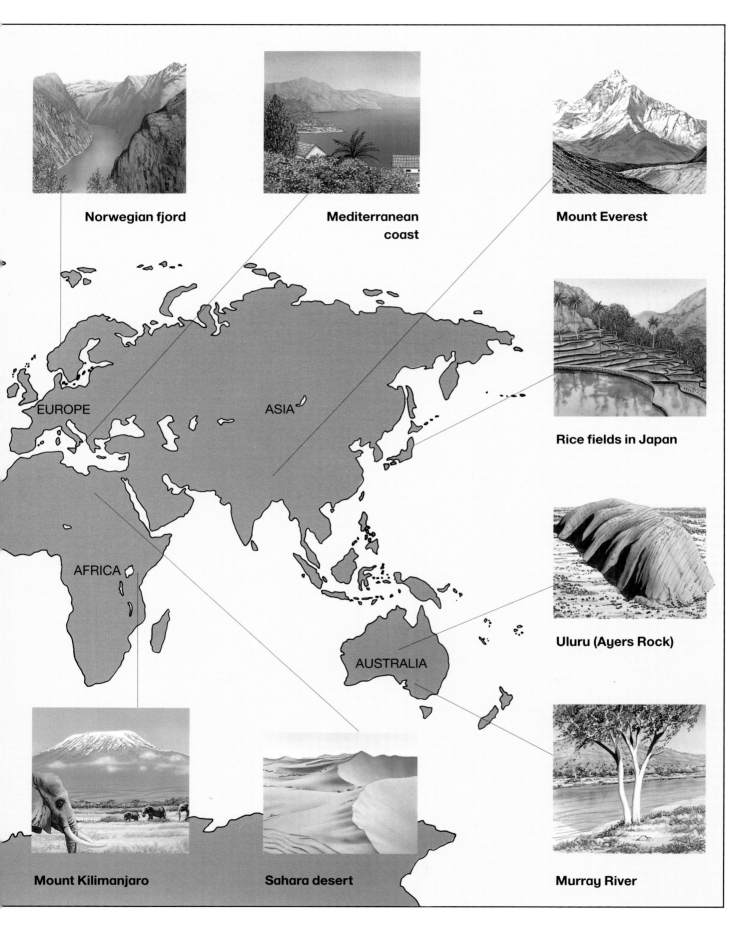

Norwegian fjord

Mediterranean coast

Mount Everest

Rice fields in Japan

EUROPE

ASIA

Uluru (Ayers Rock)

AFRICA

AUSTRALIA

Mount Kilimanjaro

Sahara desert

Murray River

Cold lands

The climate is very cold around the North and South poles. Most of the Antarctic continent, around the South Pole, is covered in thick ice all year.

The Arctic Ocean, around the North Pole, is also very cold. But in summer, snow melts on the surrounding land. Plants grow, caribou come to graze and birds come to nest.

North Pole

South Pole

△ The North and South poles are at opposite ends of the Earth. There is no day and night. In winter, it is dark all the time and in summer, it is light all the time.

Antarctic

Can you find?
1 baby Adelie penguin
2 emperor penguin
3 Adelie penguin
4 Weddell seals
5 ice-breaking ship
6 glacier

Arctic

Can you find?

1 herd of caribou
2 long-tailed skua
3 Arctic butterfly
4 Arctic poppy
5 bearberry flowers
6 male snow bunting
7 female Lapland bunting

Make ice lollies

Pour some fruit juice into clean yogurt pots. Put them in the freezer. As they start to freeze, push in a lolly stick or a plastic spoon and freeze again.

Why Polar Bear Lives on the North Pole
(Based on a story by Ted Hughes)

At one time all the animals held beauty contests to decide who was the most beautiful of them all. Polar Bear always won, which made jealous Falcon want to get rid of her. When Polar Bear became vain and hated dust on her fur, Falcon told her about the spotlessly clean North Pole. Polar Bear and her admirers, the seals, moved to the North Pole. You can still see her there today.

Forests and woods

Forests and woods grow in areas where the climate is cold in winter and warmer in summer. Evergreen trees do not lose their leaves in winter. They grow in forests in northern parts of the world, where winters are long and cold. In many countries with milder climates, there are deciduous woods. Deciduous trees lose their leaves in winter.

△ The racoon lives in the forests of North America. Racoons are good climbers. Sometimes, they raid birds' nests for the eggs. Racoons now come into towns for food.

evergreen forest

Can you find?

1 pine cone
2 grizzly bear
3 chipmunk
4 female moose
5 evergreen tree
6 lake

deciduous forest

Can you find?

1 green woodpecker
2 fox
3 acorns
4 deer
5 jay
6 deciduous tree

▽ Kookaburras live in Australia. They eat lizards, snakes and insects as well as other small animals.

Find the answers

What happens to deciduous trees in winter?

What does evergreen mean?

Fir Tree and Bramble
(Based on a story by Aesop)

Fir Tree often boasted of his height and beauty. This upset humble Bramble, who knew he was ugly. But Fir Tree soon wished he was short and ugly too, when he saw men coming to chop him down for firewood.

Grasslands

In places with long dry seasons, it is mainly grass that grows.

In Africa, many animals live on the savanna, which is grassland with some trees. It is hot all year. In the dry season the grass is brown and dry. During the short wet season it becomes lush and green.

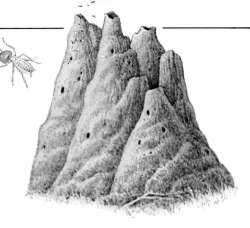

△ Termites are small insects that live in hot grasslands all over the world. They are able to build nests that are much larger than they are.

Can you find?

1 lioness and cub
2 zebras
3 gazelles
4 elephant
5 giraffes

Make a giraffe jigsaw
Trace the giraffe shown and draw it on a piece of card. Colour it in. Carefully cut the giraffe out and then cut it into several pieces. Jumble the pieces up. Can you work out where the pieces go to make the giraffe whole again?

Australia's grassland is called the bush. Kangaroos and emus feed on the grasses there.

kangaroo

emu

Hot deserts

Deserts cover large parts of the world. They get very little rain, so they have few plants and animals, just a lot of sand and rock. Wind blows the sand into huge hills called dunes.

In some deserts, plant seeds lie in the ground for years. The seeds only grow when a rainstorm gives them enough water.

△ The scorpion's tail has a very nasty sting at the end. Some scorpions' stings can kill people, but they do not usually attack unless they are annoyed.

▷ The fennec fox lives in North Africa and Arabia. Its huge ears help it listen for insects to eat and also help it to keep cool.

Find the answers

Where do cactus plants store water?

What is a camel's hump full of?

What do we call the huge hills of sand in deserts?

Can you find?
1 jerboa
2 camel train
3 desert city
4 sand dunes

Draw a sand picture

On coloured, stiff paper, draw a picture with glue. Pour sand over the glue. Tip off the spare sand to reveal your picture.

▷ Cactus plants have thick stems for storing water. They can live for months without rain.

◁ The camel is good at living in deserts. Its hump is full of fat so it can travel for days without food or water.

▷ The roadrunner lives in some of the hottest parts of the American desert. It eats mainly insects and scorpions.

Rainforests

Rainforests grow in countries that are hot and have a lot of rain. More than half the world's animals and plants live in these forests. The animals live among the thick undergrowth and tall trees. In the treetops, the branches meet and form a roof called a canopy. The world's rainforests are in danger because people are cutting them down and turning them into farmland.

△ Tree frogs have suction pads on their toes to grip twigs and leaves. Tree frogs are tiny and very colourful.

◁ Leaf-cutter ants march along the forest floor. They bite off pieces of leaf and carry them back to their nests.

Make a mask

Fold a piece of card in half. The card should be 30 cm by 20 cm. Draw half of an animal's head and colour it in. Cut it out. Make a hole at each side. Thread elastic through to finish the mask.

▷ The loris comes out at night to search for food. Its large eyes help it to see in the dark.

◁ The gibbon's long arms help it to swing from tree to tree, high up in the rainforest's canopy.

Can you find?
1 emerald tree boa
2 tapir and baby
3 howler monkey
4 crowned eagle
5 hummingbird
6 butterfly
7 ocelot
8 toucan
9 macaw

Day and night

The Earth is spinning on an imaginary line called its axis. It is this spinning that gives us day and night.

The part of the Earth facing the Sun gets sunlight. This is daytime. As Earth spins around, that part turns away from the Sun and it becomes dark. This is night time. The Earth takes 24 hours to make a whole turn.

Never look straight at the Sun. It will damage your eyes.

Word box
Axis is the imaginary line that goes through the centre of the Earth.
Poles are the two ends of the Earth's axis. The North Pole is at the north end. The South Pole is at the south end.
Equator is an imaginary line around the middle of the Earth. Places on or near the Equator are very hot.

▷ The axis is an imaginary line from the North Pole through the centre of the Earth to the South Pole. The Earth makes one whole turn every 24 hours.

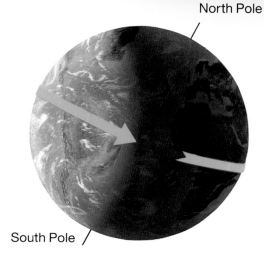

North Pole

South Pole

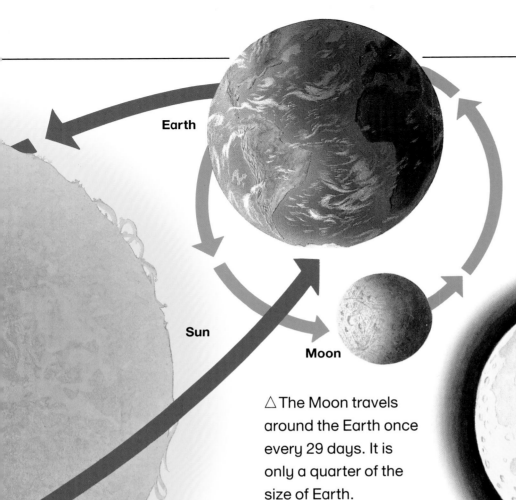

Earth

Sun

Moon

◁ As well as spinning on its axis, the Earth moves around the Sun. It takes Earth one year to travel all the way around the Sun.

△ The Moon travels around the Earth once every 29 days. It is only a quarter of the size of Earth.

Find the answers

What is an axis?

How long does the Earth take to travel once around the Sun?

Are places near the Equator hot or cold?

Day and night
Shine a torch at a ball in a dark room. The torch is the Sun. The ball is the Earth. The side facing the Sun is light, so it is day. The other side is dark, so it is night.

△ During the day, the Sun gives us light. At night time, streetlamps light the streets.

43

Seasons

The four seasons in most parts of the world are summer, autumn, winter and spring. Other places have only two seasons.

We have seasons because the Earth tilts. First one half leans towards the Sun, then the other. It is summer in the part of the world tilted towards the Sun.

Find the answers

How many seasons does the Arctic have?

When is the first day of summer in the south?

▷ June 21st is the first day of the year that land above the Equator leans towards the Sun. It is the first day of winter in the southern half of the world.

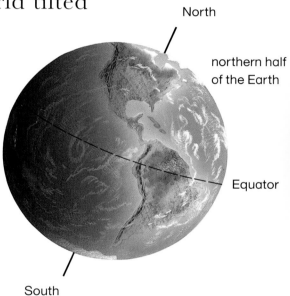

North

northern half of the Earth

Equator

South

△ In spring, days are warm and nights cool.

△ In summer, days are hot and nights warm.

△ In autumn, days and nights are cooler.

△ In winter, days and nights are cold.

△ The Arctic and Antarctic regions have just two seasons. During the summer, the sun never sets. In winter it does not rise.

△ In some places near the Equator, there are only two seasons. After the long, hot dry season, there is a wet season.

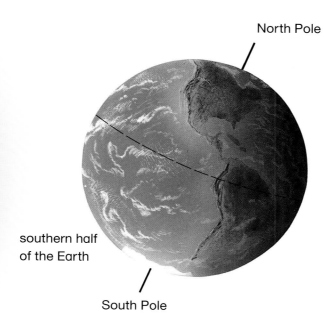

North Pole

southern half of the Earth

South Pole

◁ December 21st is the first day of the year that land below the Equator leans towards the Sun. It is the first day of winter in the northern half of the world.

Paint a summer tree
Use pencils and felt-tip pens to draw a winter tree with no leaves. Change it into a summer tree by adding leaves. Mix up different shades of green paint, and fingerprint summer leaves onto the branches.

Our blue planet

If you looked down at the Earth from Space, you would see that most of our planet is covered by water. This huge amount of water is separated into five areas, called oceans, by the land. The oceans are the Arctic, Antarctic, Atlantic, Indian and Pacific. Smaller areas of the oceans are called seas. Two of the largest seas are the Caribbean and Mediterranean.

△ There is more water than land on the Earth's surface. Nearly three-quarters of the Earth is covered in water.

▷ The oceans and seas are all joined up, so you can travel from one to the other without crossing any land. Because the Earth is round, if you set off from the Pacific Ocean and kept on sailing right, you would eventually return to the Pacific again.

Word box
Oceans are the five vast areas of salty water that surround all the land on Earth.
Plankton are tiny creatures and plants that drift in seawater and fresh water.

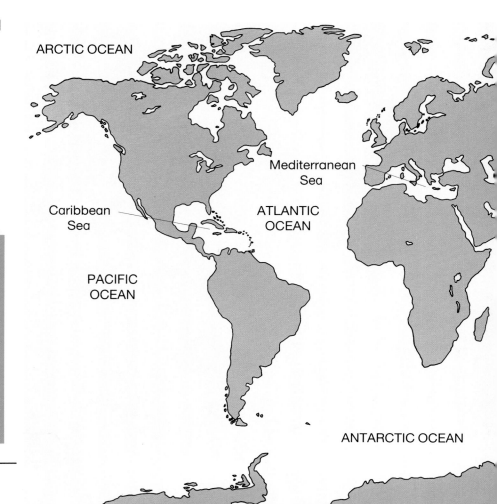

ARCTIC OCEAN

Mediterranean Sea

Caribbean Sea

ATLANTIC OCEAN

PACIFIC OCEAN

ANTARCTIC OCEAN

▽ Life on Earth began in the sea millions of years ago. Now it is home to many plants and animals, from tiny plankton to the huge blue whales that feed on them.

plankton

blue whale

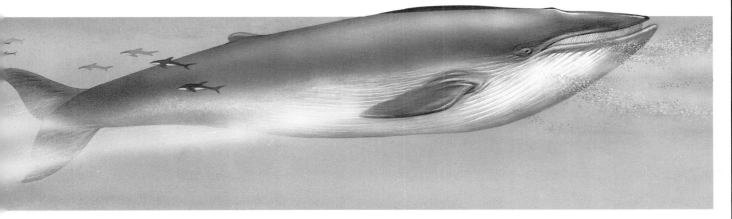

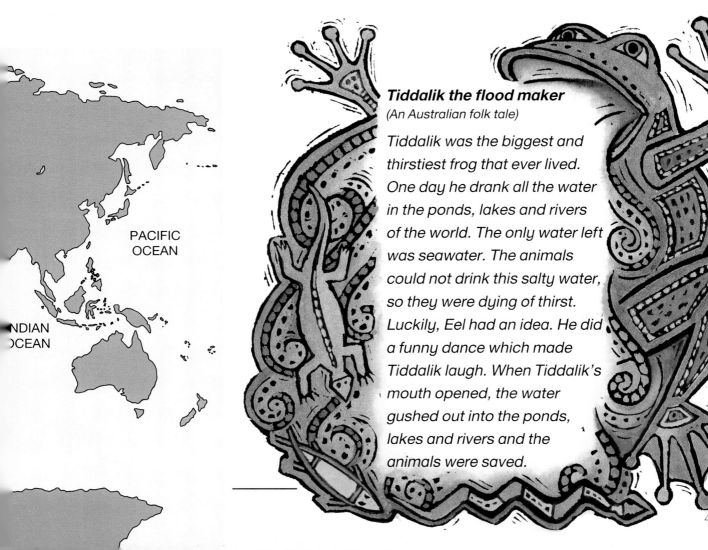

PACIFIC OCEAN

NDIAN OCEAN

Tiddalik the flood maker
(An Australian folk tale)

Tiddalik was the biggest and thirstiest frog that ever lived. One day he drank all the water in the ponds, lakes and rivers of the world. The only water left was seawater. The animals could not drink this salty water, so they were dying of thirst. Luckily, Eel had an idea. He did a funny dance which made Tiddalik laugh. When Tiddalik's mouth opened, the water gushed out into the ponds, lakes and rivers and the animals were saved.

47

Waves and tides

The sea is never still. Waves and tides keep the water moving. Most waves are made by the wind. The stronger the wind, the bigger the waves. They are fun for surfing on, but dangerous for ships out at sea.

Twice a day the tides come in and go out. At high tide the water moves further onto the land. At low tide, it moves away from the land.

King Canute and the tides
Long ago lived a King called Canute. People believed he could do anything, even stop the tides. But he showed them that no one can stop the tides.

wind

▽ In a storm, strong winds blowing across the top of the sea make huge waves with foamy edges. These waves are called whitecaps.

Find the answers

What happens at high tide?

What starts a tsunami?

What is a whitecap?

48

Make waves in the bath

Waves look as if they go forward, but really they only move up and down. To see this, put a toy into the bath and make some waves with your hands. The toy will bob up and down on the waves.

▽ When the water near to the shore rises and gets deeper it is high tide. When the water falls, it is low tide. Boats in a harbour may be left sitting on the mud at low tide.

▽ Waves called tsunamis (soo-nah-mees) can cause a lot of damage to the land. They are started by underwater earthquakes and volcanoes.

49

Zones

Sea animals live in different zones, or areas, of the sea. Some zones are deeper than others. Most animals and plants live in the top zone, where it is warm. Here, there is enough sunlight for plants to grow. Not many animals are able to live at the bottom of the sea where it is cold and dark.

▷ Animals that hunt other animals are called predators. They usually live in the same zone as their prey, the animals that they eat. Creatures living in the bottom zone also eat bits of food that fall down from above.

Word box
Predators are animals that hunt and kill other animals for food.
Prey are the animals hunted by predators.

Find the answers

What are prey?

Where do sea plants grow?

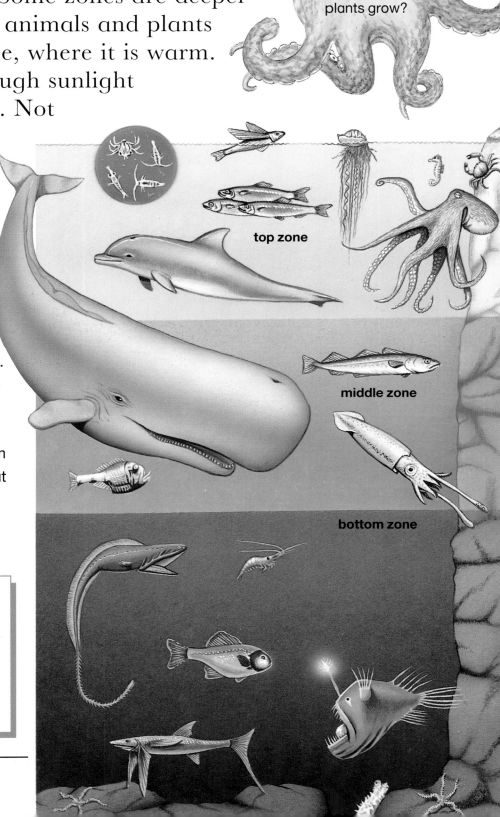

top zone

middle zone

bottom zone

50

Plankton

Plankton are the smallest living things in the sea. They live near the surface of the water and are food for many sea animals. Some plankton are plants and others are animals. Animal plankton eat plant plankton.

△ Most plankton are so small that you can see them only with a microscope.

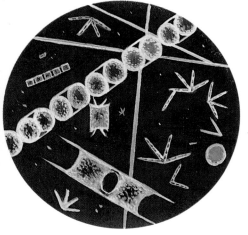

plant plankton
under a microscope

animal plankton
under a microscope

▷ Blue whales, the largest animals in the sea, feed on animal plankton. One whale can eat four tonnes a day!

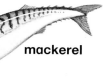

mackerel

jellyfish

sea anemone

△ Sea anemones, jellyfish and fish, such as mackerel, eat plankton.

Saving the sea

The sea is beautiful and valuable. Everyone should do all they can to help protect it. Many people are trying to stop the harm we are doing to the sea. The world is beginning to realize how important the sea is, but there is still a lot to do. What can you do?

▷ You and your friends could start by clearing up your own rubbish when you visit the seashore.

△ If you look at a globe you will see just how much of our planet is covered by the sea. Do you know which is the largest ocean?

▽ The sea is a wonderful place to have fun. The best beaches are clean beaches.

△ You could learn more about the sea. Then you will know how to protect it.

All Kinds
of Animals

What is an animal?

Animals are living things. So are plants. They both need energy to live, but they get their energy in different ways. Plants use the sun's energy. Animals cannot do that. Animals get their energy from the food they eat. Some animals eat plants, some eat other animals, and some eat plants and animals. There are many different kinds of animal. Scientists arrange them in groups.

△ Animals come in many shapes and sizes, from tiny snails to big giraffes. They all breathe and feed and grow.

the frog is an amphibian

the swallow is a bird

the mouse is a mammal

the cricket is an insect

Word box
Vertebrates are animals with backbones as part of their skeletons.
Invertebrates are animals without backbones. Some have a hard outside, a bit like armour. This is called an external skeleton.

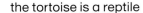

the tortoise is a reptile

the stickleback is a fish

▽ These animals are all mammals. They are more closely related to each other than to birds or reptiles or fish. Can you find mammals on the chart below?

the fox is a mammal

human beings are mammals

the zebra is a mammal

the panda is a mammal

Tiny animals

Many animals are so small that we need a powerful microscope to see them.

animal under a microscope

▽ There are over a million different kinds of animal. Scientists divide them into two main groups. Animals with backbones are called vertebrates. Animals without backbones are called invertebrates.

4,000
amphibians

4,150
mammals

6,500
reptiles

8,800
birds

21,500
fish

over
1 million

Vertebrates

Invertebrates

55

What is a mammal?

A mammal is an animal with hair or fur. This often helps to keep its body warm. Young mammals are fed with milk produced by their mother's body.

Mammals live almost everywhere, from freezing cold Antarctica to scorching hot Africa. Most mammals live on the land. Some, such as whales, live in water. Bats are the only mammals that can fly.

Find the answers

Which mammals can fly?

What do rabbits use their whiskers for?

We are mammals too
Human beings are mammals. We are fed with our mother's milk when young. All mammals are warm-blooded – their body temperature remains the same all the time, even though the temperature of their surroundings may change.

Word box
Herbivore is an animal that eats only plants.
Carnivore is an animal that eats other animals.

◁ Mammals often give birth to several young at once.

▽ Most mammals are good at seeing, hearing and smelling things around them. Rabbits use whiskers to feel things, too.

Design a mammal game
Each player think of a mammal. Draw its head at the top of a page. Fold over and pass onto next player. Draw the top half of the mammal's body, then its lower body and feet. Fold over and pass on each time. Open papers out to find new mammals.

hair or fur

whiskers

most mammals move on four legs

▷ Most mammals give birth to live babies, but the platypus lays eggs with leathery shells.

◁ Some mammals hibernate. They eat a great deal in the autumn, then curl up and sleep through the cold winter. This dormouse will not wake up until spring.

What is a bird?

A bird is an animal with feathers and wings. Birds live in most parts of the world, and nearly all of them can fly.

The smallest bird is the bee hummingbird, which is only five centimetres long. The largest is the ostrich, which can grow to two and a half metres tall.

birds' ears are on either side of their head hidden by feathers

pigeon

The Ugly Duckling
(A story by Hans Andersen)

The cruel animals teased the Ugly Duckling for his ugliness. But by spring, he had grown into a beautiful swan.

Word box
Preening is the way a bird keeps itself clean. A bird preens its feathers with its beak.
Birds of prey are birds that hunt other animals for food.

Print a peacock
Using bright paints, make hand prints on paper. When dry, cut them out and glue in a fan shape to make a peacock's tail. Cut out a body and glue it in the middle of your picture.

beak or bill

birds have two feet
with claws for gripping

**Canada
geese**

△ When a bird flaps its wings,
its feathers push the air back
and down, so the bird moves
forward and up.

ostrich

△ A few birds, such as the
huge ostrich, cannot fly. But
the ostrich can run very fast.

What is a reptile?

Crocodiles, snakes, lizards, tortoises and turtles are all reptiles. Reptiles are cold-blooded animals. This means that they cannot keep their bodies warm in cold weather. They need lots of sunshine to keep warm, so most reptiles live in hot countries. Reptiles that live in cold countries sleep all winter and wake up in spring. This is called hibernation.

gila monster

△ Reptiles bask in the sun to get warm. If a reptile gets too hot, it hurries into the shade or into some cool water.

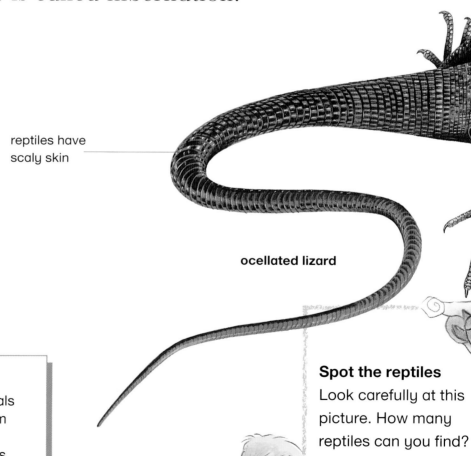

reptiles have scaly skin

ocellated lizard

Word box
Warm-blooded animals keep themselves warm by eating.
Cold-blooded animals need heat from the sun to keep warm.

Spot the reptiles
Look carefully at this picture. How many reptiles can you find?

marine turtle

△ Some reptiles live longer than any other animal. Large turtles and tortoises can live for more than 100 years.

Find the answers

Is a crocodile a reptile?

How do reptiles get warm?

Are reptiles' eggs hard like birds' eggs?

many reptiles are brightly coloured

◁ Geckos have sucker like pads on their feet. This helps them to run up walls when hunting for insects.

▷ This king snake is hatching from its egg. Reptiles' eggs are not hard like birds' eggs, but soft and leathery.

▷ As it grows, a king snake will shed its skin. It has a brand new skin underneath. The snake rubs its head against something rough until the old skin splits open. Then the snake wriggles out.

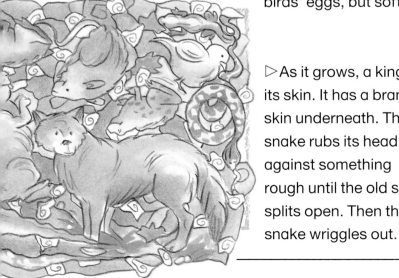

61

What is an amphibian?

An amphibian is an animal that lives both in water and on land. Frogs, toads, newts and salamanders are amphibians. Amphibians lay their eggs in water, perhaps in a pond or stream. Amphibians cannot live in salt water, so there are none in the sea.

Find the answers

Where do tadpoles live?

What is an amphibian?

Is a newt an amphibian?

great crested newt

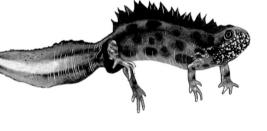

▷Newts and salamanders are amphibians. Unlike frogs or toads, they do not lose their tails when they grow up.

long-tailed salamander

alpine salamander

frogs and toads have two strong back legs for jumping and swimming

Word box
Amphibians are animals that spend part of their life in water and part on land.
Tadpoles turn into frogs or toads after losing their tails and developing legs.

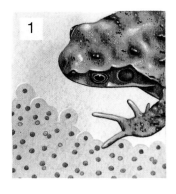 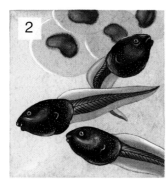  

△ Female frogs lay hundreds of small eggs in water. The eggs hatch into tadpoles, with long tails. To start with, tadpoles only eat plants.

△ The tadpoles get bigger and begin to grow legs. Their tails shrink, and after about four months, the baby frogs can leave the water.

amphibians have two eyes that can see all around them

▽ Male frogs and toads puff up their throats with air and let out a big, loud croak.

reed frog

European green toad

Frog jumping race
Can you jump like a frog? Squat down and stretch your arms to the floor. Leap forward with a powerful jump. Have a frog race with your friends.

What is a fish?

A fish spends its whole life in water. Some fish live in the sea, and some in rivers and lakes. Their bodies are usually covered with scales.

Like all animals, fish need oxygen to live. We get oxygen from air, but fish get it from water. Water enters the fish's mouth and passes over its gills, which take in the oxygen. The water then goes out through gill slits.

◁ Most fish lay eggs, often thousands at a time. The eggs have no shells, and many are eaten by other fish. Only a few hatch.

▽ The butterflyfish has a big spot like an eye to confuse its enemies.

herring

a tail helps most fish push through water

scale

The Little Mermaid
Hans Andersen wrote a story about a mermaid. Mermaids are imaginary sea creatures. They are like humans, but have a fish's tail instead of legs.

eel

64

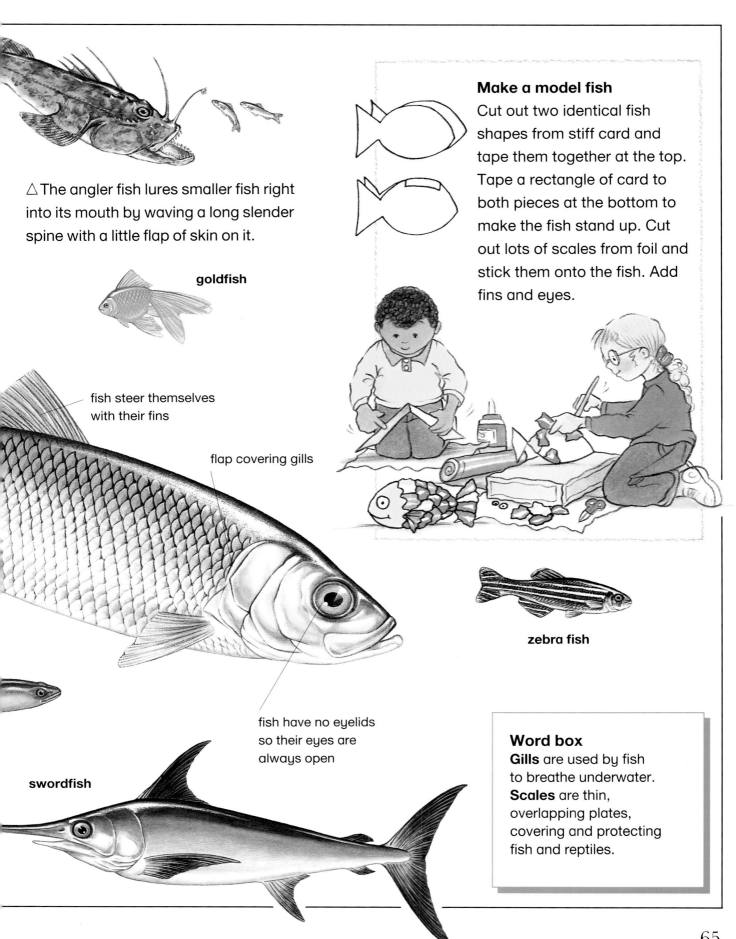

△ The angler fish lures smaller fish right into its mouth by waving a long slender spine with a little flap of skin on it.

goldfish

fish steer themselves with their fins

flap covering gills

fish have no eyelids so their eyes are always open

swordfish

Make a model fish
Cut out two identical fish shapes from stiff card and tape them together at the top. Tape a rectangle of card to both pieces at the bottom to make the fish stand up. Cut out lots of scales from foil and stick them onto the fish. Add fins and eyes.

zebra fish

Word box
Gills are used by fish to breathe underwater. **Scales** are thin, overlapping plates, covering and protecting fish and reptiles.

What is an insect?

Insects have six legs. Their bodies have a hard outer case called an exoskeleton. Every insect's body has three parts: a head, a thorax or middle and an abdomen at the back.

Most insects can fly. Usually, insects have two pairs of wings. All flies, however, have only one pair of wings.

Insects are often brightly coloured to warn other animals not to eat them because they taste nasty.

△ This ladybird has two pairs of wings. The front wings are hard, and they cover the delicate back wings when the ladybird is not flying.

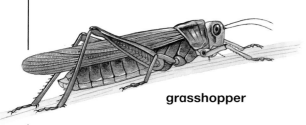

grasshopper

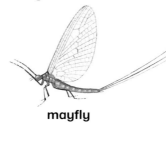

mayfly

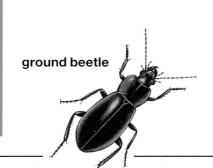

housefly

ground beetle

an insect's legs and wings are attached to the thorax

Word box
Antennae are the two feelers on the heads of small creatures, such as insects.
Metamorphosis is the complete change that happens to some creatures' bodies before they become adults.

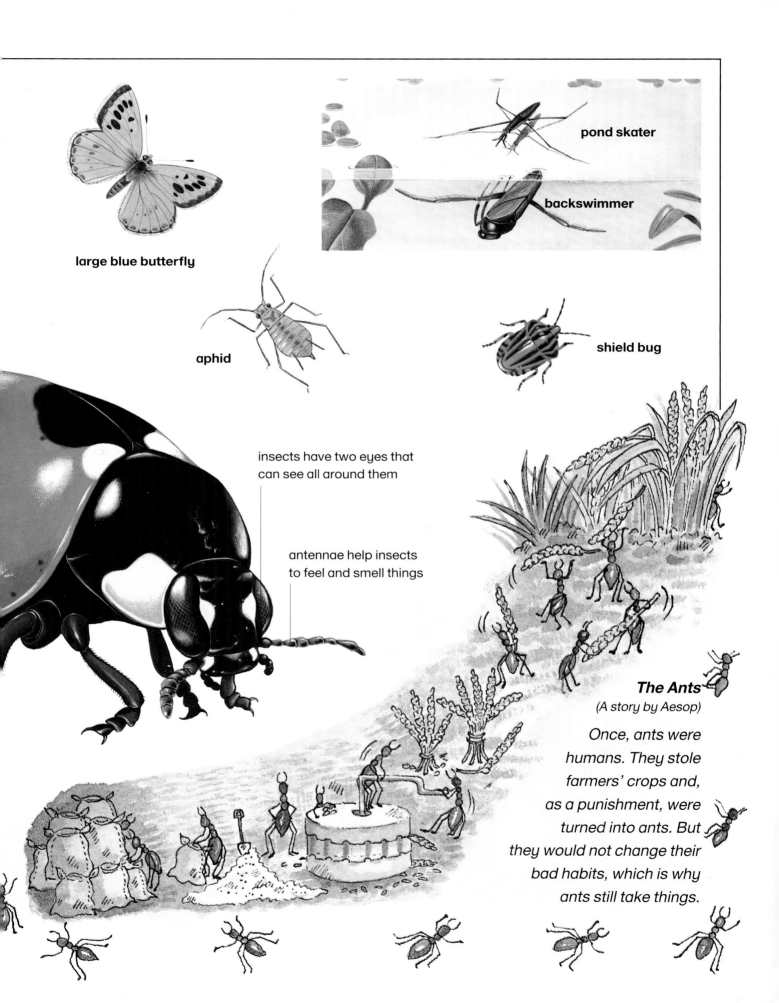

large blue butterfly

pond skater

backswimmer

aphid

shield bug

insects have two eyes that can see all around them

antennae help insects to feel and smell things

The Ants
(A story by Aesop)

Once, ants were humans. They stole farmers' crops and, as a punishment, were turned into ants. But they would not change their bad habits, which is why ants still take things.

Butterflies

Some of the most beautiful insects are butterflies. Their wings are covered with tiny, overlapping scales which give the wings their bright colours.

Butterflies, like many insects, go through several different stages before becoming adults. This change in their bodies is called metamorphosis.

△ The swallowtail butterfly lays eggs on a plant that her babies will be able to eat.

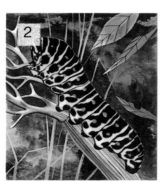
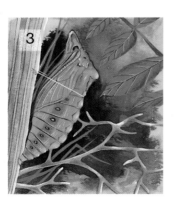
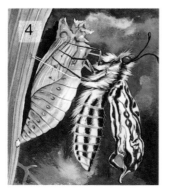

△ A caterpillar hatches out of each butterfly egg. Caterpillars eat a lot and grow quickly. The caterpillar turns into a chrysalis. Out of this crawls a beautiful butterfly.

Make butterfly prints

Fold a piece of paper in half.

Open it up and put spots of paint on one side. Refold and press down. Open out. When dry, paint a body and two antennae to complete a butterfly picture.

Plants

Plants are alive

Plants are living things. They need food to give them energy. Plants make their own food by taking in water from the soil through their roots. The water travels up the stem to the leaves. The leaves contain a green colouring called chlorophyll. With sunlight, chlorophyll helps change the water into food.

▽ Plants need water to live. They take it in through their roots. The water travels through their stems to the veins in their leaves.

vein

stem

root

bell jar

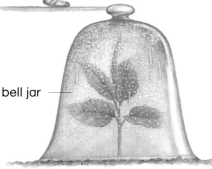

△ People sweat, and so do plants. Some of the water soaked up by the roots is given off by the leaves. You can see this if you place a plant inside a bell jar.

Make a potato maze
Make a hole in the end of a cardboard box. Stick cardboard inside to make a maze, as shown. Put a sprouting potato at the end of the maze. Put the lid on. Leave in a light place. See a shoot grow out of the hole, towards the light.

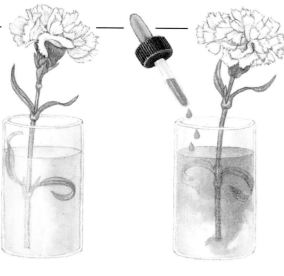

white flower **add colouring** **pink flower**

◁ Here is a way to show that water travels right through a plant. Put a white flower in water. Add some red food colouring to the water. The flower will take up the coloured water. After a few hours it will turn pink. The water has moved up the stem and into the leaves and petals.

△ A pot plant needs light, air, soil and water to survive.

△ Cut flowers survive in just water, but only for a few days.

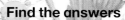

Find the answers

What do pot plants need to live?

How do plants take up water?

△ Plants wither and die if they are left in the dark.

△ Plants dry out and die if they are uprooted from the soil.

Word box
Chlorophyll is a green colouring found in the leaves of plants. It uses sunlight to make food for plants.
Veins are the tiny tubes in the leaves of plants.

Making new plants

Flowers make the seeds that grow into new plants. Each flower has male parts, called stamens, and female parts, called carpels. The stamens produce grains called pollen. For a plant to make seeds, pollen must reach the carpels. This is called pollination. It happens in several different ways.

▽ Look closely at the centre of a sunflower. You will see that it is made up of many small flowers. Each has a carpel.

carpel

lords-and-ladies

▷Insects climb down to the nectar at the bottom of the lords-and-ladies plant. On the way, pollen from the stamens stick to them. If this pollen rubs off onto the carpel, pollination occurs.

stamen

carpel

nectar

fuchsia

lily

stamens

◁ The stamens of the fuchsia and the lily are easy to see. They are on long stalks. Insects visit the flowers because they like their colour and smell.

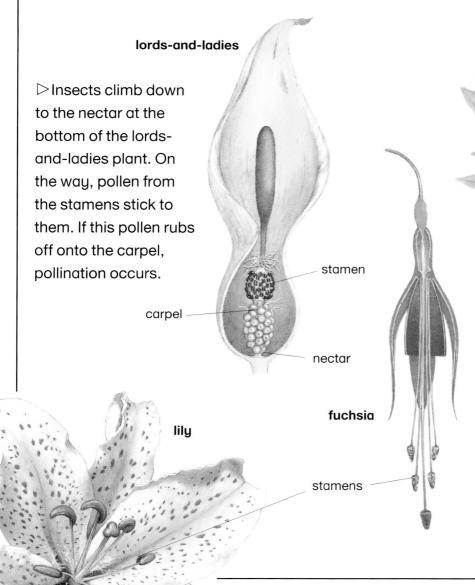

cone

◁ Pine trees make pollen in little yellow male cones. The wind blows the pollen from the male cones on one tree to the female cones on another.

stamen

carpel

leaf

inner petal

stamen

carpel

outer petals

△ Sometimes pollen travels from the stamens to the carpels of the same flower. This is called self-pollination.

▽ This dog rose is pollinated by a bee. Pollen sticks to the bee's furry body on one flower. Then it brushes off on another flower.

Make a flower
Trace the shapes onto very thin, coloured card. Cut out five inner petals, the outer petals, five stamens, one carpel, two leaves. Poke a bendy straw through the outer petals. Push the petal ends into the straw, then the carpel and stamens. Tape on leaves.

73

From flower to fruit

Inside the carpels there are little eggs called ovules. When pollen reaches an ovule, a seed starts to grow. Then a fruit grows around the seed. This is to protect the seed as it grows. Some fruits have one seed inside a hard stone. Other fruits have several seeds, called pips, in juicy pulp.

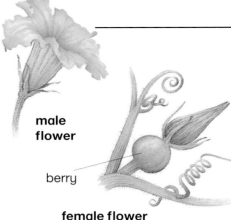

male flower

berry

female flower

△ The pumpkin plant has male and female flowers. After pollination, each female flower grows a fruit called a berry.

▷ Rose hips are the fruits of the dog rose. They contain a lot of small seeds. As soon as the fruit starts to grow, the petals of the dog rose drop off. The rose hips turn from green to red.

rose hip

▽ The berry grows into a big orange pumpkin. The pumpkin has thick, juicy flesh. In the centre of the pumpkin there are lots of small seeds.

pumpkin

pear

△ After pollination, tiny fruits grow underneath the pear flowers. The petals drop off and the fruits begin to swell.

△ The fruits grow bigger. Some drop off. Others become ripe pears. Inside are small seeds called pips.

Chicken-Licken
(An English folk tale)

A nut fell on Chicken-Licken's head. She thought it was the sky falling down. She told the other birds and they went to warn the king. But on the way, they met cunning Foxy-Loxy. He tricked them by saying his den was a short cut to the palace. Then he ate them all.

sloes

peach

▷These are all fruits with stones. They have only one large seed inside.

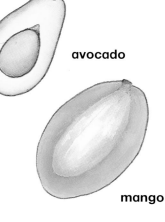
avocado

mango

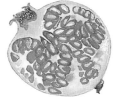
bilberries

passion fruit

pomegranate

kiwi fruit

△ These are fruits with pips. They have a lot of small seeds inside them.

Make a dried seed picture
Use dried peas, lentils, sunflower seeds and haricot beans.

Do not use red kidney beans. They are poisonous before they are cooked.

Draw a simple picture on a piece of paper. Glue on different coloured seeds. You could make a face, a bird, or an animal.

▷These are nuts. They are seeds with a hard shell around them.

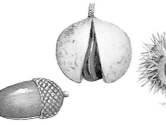

◁ The poppy holds its seeds inside a case with a lid. It has lots of tiny seeds.

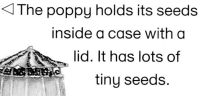

Ready for a journey

Seeds need to reach the ground to grow into new plants. They travel in different ways. Some fall straight to earth. Others are carried by wind, or water, or by birds and other animals. Once the seeds are buried in soil and watered, they begin to swell. A plant begins to grow out of the seed. The root grows first and then a shoot. This is called germination.

▷When birds eat fruit, they spit out the seeds or swallow them. Some seeds reach the ground in the bird droppings.

△Dandelion seeds are scattered by the wind.

▽ Honesty seeds are flung out when the pods burst open.

◁Some fruits have tiny hooks and spines. They stick to the coats of animals. Sometimes they are carried a long way.

Jack and the beanstalk
(An English folk tale)

Jack planted a magic bean. It grew into a huge beanstalk. He climbed to the top and found the castle of a wicked giant. He took some gold. Then he took a hen that laid golden eggs. The giant found out and chased him down the beanstalk. Jack chopped the stalk with an axe. The giant fell down dead.

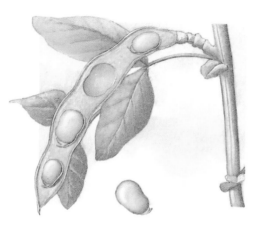

△ Broad beans are good to eat. The beans from the pod are seeds and can also be used to grow new plants.

△ The gardener puts the beans in the soil and covers them. Then the soil is watered.

△ Soon little bean plants appear. The plants will grow quickly with sun and water.

Grow runner beans

Soak runner bean seeds in water overnight. Take a jam jar and cut a piece of blotting paper to fit around the inside. Crumple paper towels in the middle. Push beans between the blotting paper and the side of the jar. Water the towel just enough to keep the blotting paper damp. Put the jar in a warm, dark place. When roots and shoots appear, put the jar upright by a sunny window.

▽ When a bean germinates, a small root appears first. It grows downwards. Then a leafy shoot appears. It pushes upwards towards the light. More leaves and flowers appear above the soil.

leaf

shoot

root

The seasons

There are four seasons. They are spring, summer, autumn and winter. The weather changes and this affects the way plants grow. Leaves, flowers and fruit come and go as the seasons change. Not all parts of the world have four seasons. Some places have only one or two.

△ Many plants lose their leaves in the cold of winter.

△ In spring, it gets warmer and new leaves start to grow.

△ In summer, trees are in full leaf. The weather is warm.

△ The tomato seed is sown at the end of winter.

△ During the spring, a young plant grows.

△ In summer, the plant flowers. Then small fruits appear.

The Secret Garden
(A story by Frances Hodgson Burnett)

Two children find a secret garden. In winter, they work hard to clear and plant it. In spring, the flowers look beautiful.

△ In the tropical rainforests near the Equator, it stays hot and wet all year round. These rainforests are always green. There is only one season here.

short rainy season

△ In the desert, there is a long dry season and a short rainy season. When the rain comes, some plants sprout, flower and make seeds very quickly.

△ In autumn, it gets cooler. The leaves start to fall.

△ In autumn, the fruits ripen and are picked.

Make a cactus
Take a rectangle of corrugated paper or card. Bend it round to form a tube. Glue the sides together. Paint it green. Fill a flower pot with sand and stand the cactus in it. Cut some paper flowers from coloured paper. Glue them on the cactus. Put small stones on the sand.

Plants in danger

Many plants are in danger. Pollution, fires, new roads and buildings can damage the places where plants live. Huge areas of forest are cleared for farming each year. Some plants are in danger of becoming extinct. That means they may disappear for ever.

△ When a fire breaks out, firefighting aircraft spray water and chemicals over the forest to put out the flames.

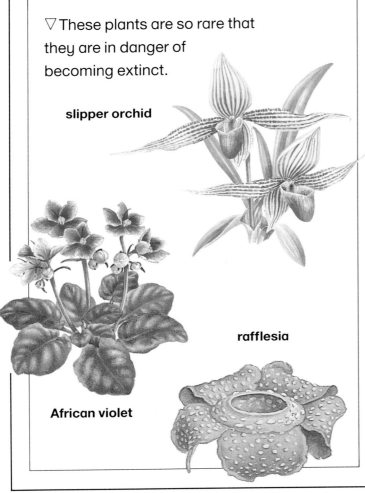

▽ These plants are so rare that they are in danger of becoming extinct.

slipper orchid

rafflesia

African violet

△ Many forests are being destroyed to provide timber and make room for farmland.

When Dinosaurs Lived

Meeting dinosaurs

Dinosaurs lived on Earth millions of years ago. Then they became extinct, which means they died out for ever. They were extinct long before people lived, so no one has ever seen a live dinosaur.

We know a great deal about dinosaurs because people have found fossils of their bones and teeth. Often the bones make up whole skeletons which can be put on show in museums.

a long tail helped this enormous dinosaur to balance

▷This skeleton belonged to one of the fiercest dinosaurs of all, Tyrannosaurus rex. Scientists studied the different bones and found out about how Tyrannosaurus lived.

Word box
Fossils are the remains of animals and plants that lived long ago. They are usually found hardened in rock.
Palaeontologists are people who study fossils.

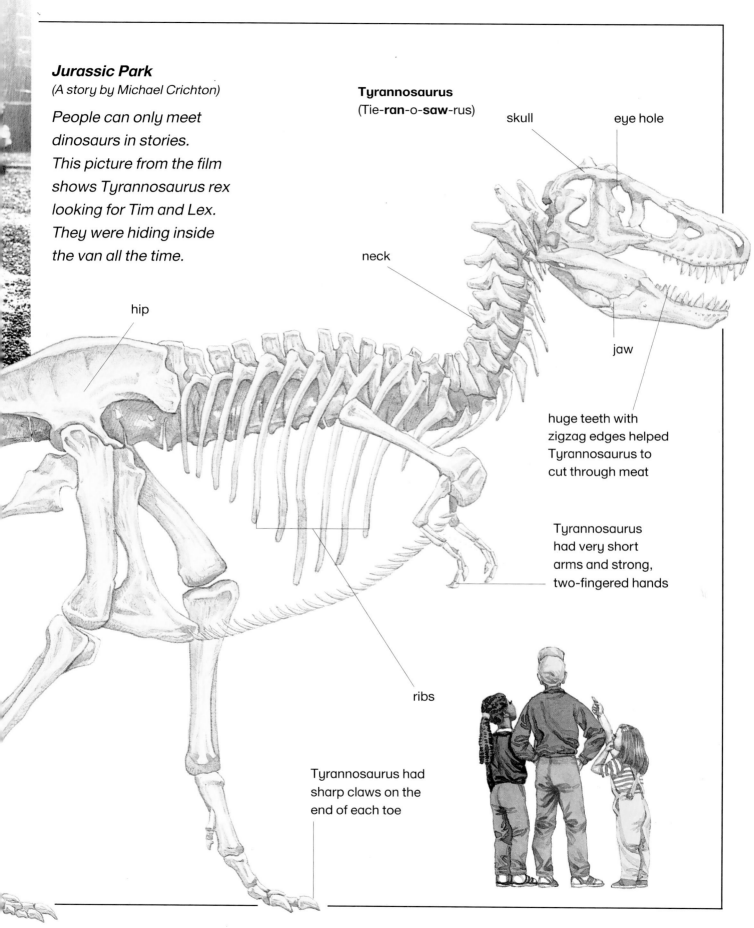

Jurassic Park
(A story by Michael Crichton)

People can only meet dinosaurs in stories. This picture from the film shows Tyrannosaurus rex looking for Tim and Lex. They were hiding inside the van all the time.

Tyrannosaurus
(Tie-**ran**-o-**saw**-rus)

skull

eye hole

neck

jaw

hip

huge teeth with zigzag edges helped Tyrannosaurus to cut through meat

Tyrannosaurus had very short arms and strong, two-fingered hands

ribs

Tyrannosaurus had sharp claws on the end of each toe

Different dinosaurs

Dinosaurs were all different shapes and sizes. Some were huge. Others were the size of a turkey. Some plodded on all fours. Others walked and ran on their back legs. There were fierce meat-eaters and gentle plant-eaters. Scientists believe that dinosaurs were reptiles, so they all had scaly skin and laid eggs.

Apatosaurus
(A-**pat**-o-**saw**-rus)

Apatosaurus prints
Some Apatosaurus footprints were found in Mexico. Before this, scientists thought that Apatosaurus had been too heavy to live on land and must have needed water to support its great weight.

Coelophysis
(**See**-lo-**fie**-sis)

△ Coelophysis was one of the first dinosaurs to have lived. It was about the size of a ten-year-old child.

▽ Diplodocus was one of the longest dinosaurs. It had a tiny skull compared to its huge body.

Word box
Reptiles are cold-blooded animals that use heat from the sun to keep warm. They lay eggs.
Camouflage is a way of hiding. Animals use their shape and colour to blend in with their surroundings.

▽ Compsognathus is the smallest known dinosaur. It had sharp little teeth and could run very fast to catch lizards to eat.

Compsognathus
(Komp-**sog**-nath-us)

Diplodocus
(Dip-**lod**-o-kus)

Make a dough dinosaur
Make dough using the recipe and instructions at the beginning of this book. Add some food colouring. Mould the dough into your favourite dinosaur shapes. Roll out a thick sausage of dough for the larger dinosaurs' necks.

▽ Some of the largest dinosaurs, such as Seismosaurus and Brachiosaurus, were plant-eaters. Seismosaurus was the biggest dinosaur. Its name means earthshaker. Tyrannosaurus rex was the biggest meat-eater ever. If it were alive today, it could peer into upstairs windows!

Seismosaurus
(**Size**-mo-**saw**-rus)

Brachiosaurus

Tyrannosaurus

Sorting dinosaurs

Scientists use dinosaurs' hip bones to sort them into two groups. If the hip bone points forwards, it is a lizard hip. If it points backwards, it is a bird hip.

Skin prints show that dinosaurs had different kinds of skin. Some had big, knobbly plates and others had small, smooth scales. We can only guess what colour their skin was. Maybe they were the same colour as modern reptiles.

A mix-up
A Camarasaurus' head was put on the first Apatosaurus fossil found. Scientists called the dinosaur Brontosaurus. This was a mistake. We now know that this mixed-up Brontosaurus never existed.

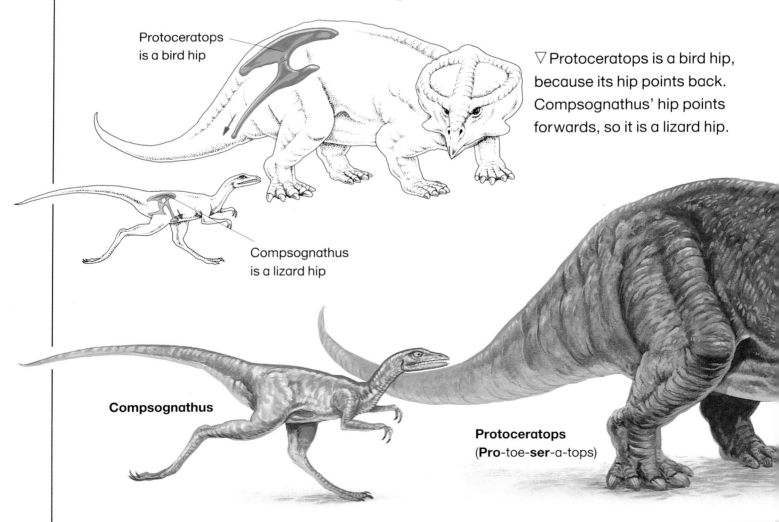

Protoceratops
is a bird hip

Compsognathus
is a lizard hip

▽ Protoceratops is a bird hip, because its hip points back. Compsognathus' hip points forwards, so it is a lizard hip.

Compsognathus

Protoceratops
(**Pro**-toe-**ser**-a-tops)

▷Fossilized skin prints do not show us what colour dinosaurs were. Perhaps they were different colours for different reasons, just like reptiles today.

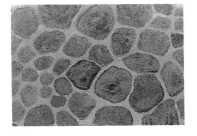

Ankylosaurus
(An-**kill**-o-**saw**-rus)

Diplodocus

coral snake

desert snake

△Coral snakes have bright stripes to warn off meat-eaters. Their poison can kill. Desert snakes are a dull colour. They can hide in the sand.

◁The modern collared lizards have different markings to show which is male and which is female. Perhaps male dinosaurs had different colourings from females.

female

male

▷Young alligators are stripy. Their stripes camouflage, or hide them, among the grasses.

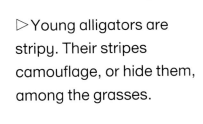

baby alligator

▽Adult alligators are a different colour. They are camouflaged when they lie in muddy rivers.

adult alligator

Dinosaur lives

Some dinosaurs grew up and lived in large groups called herds. The dinosaurs in the herd protected one another. No one is exactly sure how long dinosaurs lived. Scientists think that some reached an amazing age of 200 years old, but many died from injury or disease before that.

Draw a zigzag scene
Draw two pictures the same size. One has a dinosaur alone, the other has the dinosaur with the rest of its herd.

Parasaurolophus
(**Par**-a-**saw**-ro-**lof**-us)

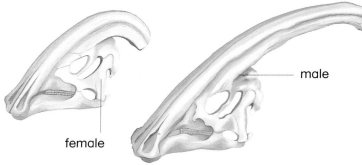

male

female

◁ Skulls show that the male Parasaurolophus had a longer crest than the female. Male dinosaurs may have used their crests and horns for showing off to the females.

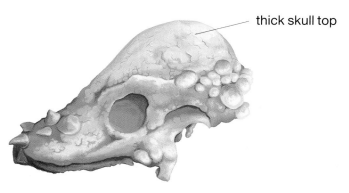

thick skull top

▷ Pachycephalosaurus had a thick skull top. The males probably crashed heads in fights to win a female, just as stags use antlers today.

Pachycephalosaurus
(**Pak**-ee-**kef**-a-lo-**saw**-rus)

Fold pictures into zigzag pleats. Cut folds to make strips. Paste strips alternately onto a piece of paper. Fold into a zigzag pleat.

Look from one side, then the other. What can you see?

▽ A fierce Tyrannosaurus is attacking this herd of Triceratops. The babies and the weaker animals huddle together in the middle. The big males stand around the herd to protect them. They point their horns outwards, ready to fight.

Corythosaurus

Corythosaurus had hollow pipes inside their head domes. Some people think they used these to make loud sounds that could warn other herd members of danger.

Corythosaurus
(**Ko-ree**-tho-**saw**-rus)

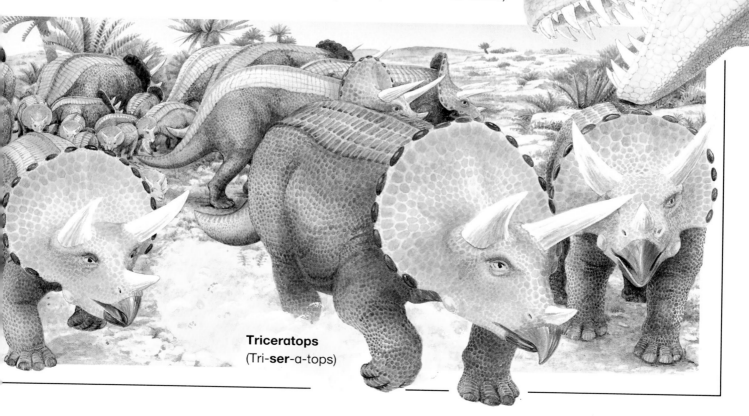

Triceratops
(Tri-**ser**-a-tops)

On the move

Dinosaurs may have swum to cross a river, but they spent their time eating, sleeping and raising their young on dry land. Fossil footprints show how dinosaurs moved. From these we can tell whether a dinosaur was travelling alone or in a herd. We can also tell how fast they travelled. These footprints are found worldwide.

Find the answers

Who left behind three-toed prints?

How do we know some dinosaurs travelled in herds?

◁ Iguanodon usually walked on all fours, but rose on its back legs to move faster.

▷ Megalosaurus left huge, three-toed footprints. They show that it always went around on its back legs.

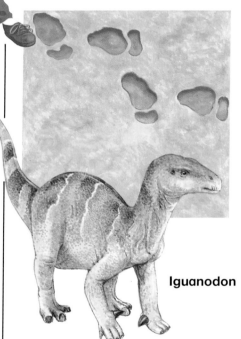

Iguanodon

Megalosaurus
(**Meg**-a-lo-**saw**-rus)

Struthiomimus
(**Strooth**-ee-o-**mime**-us)

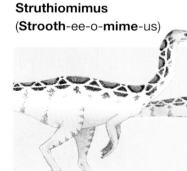

▷ By looking at the length of its legs and footprints, we know that Struthiomimus ran as fast as a racehorse. The faster an animal runs, the bigger the spaces between its footprints, or tracks.

△ Many plant-eating dinosaurs travelled long distances in herds of up to a hundred animals, looking for grazing places. Some tracks seem to show that the young animals walked in the middle of the herd, safe from attack.

▷ These Apatosaurus prints were all made at the same time. This proves that some dinosaurs moved in herds.

Dinosaur race
Cut out cardboard dinosaur shapes like the one shown here. Make a hole in each one's head. Tie string to an equal number of chairs at the far end of a room. Thread the dinosaurs onto the string and move the string up and down to race them.

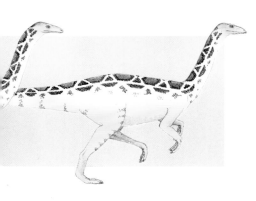

Looking for food

Some dinosaurs were herbivores. That means they ate only plants. Others were carnivores. They ate meat. The many known kinds of plant-eater fed on leaves, cones and roots. Often the meat-eaters with their large, strong jaws and sharp teeth would attack and eat these peaceful animals.

▽ Edmontosaurus was a plant-eating dinosaur. It had hundreds of teeth in a huge jaw which helped it eat tough leaves and roots.

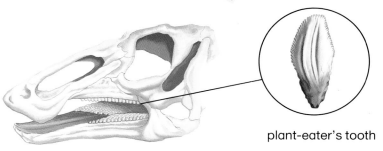

plant-eater's tooth

Edmontosaurus
(**Ed**-mont-o-**saw**-rus)

△ Edmontosaurus' skull had a bony beak at the front, for nipping bits off a plant. Its teeth were worn down by all the chewing, so new teeth were always growing.

▽ Some plant-eaters swallowed stones, just as birds swallow grit, to help grind up and digest the food in their stomachs.

Make dinosaur plant food

Roll up a newspaper tightly. Secure the middle and bottom with rubber bands. Make four cuts as far as the first band. Pull the middle of the roll out, to make a plant for a dinosaur.

Coelophysis the cannibal
Scientists found a baby Coelophysis inside an adult of the same kind. So some dinosaurs were cannibals, which means they ate each other!

▽ Meat-eaters' teeth were different from the plant-eaters'. The edges were like tiny saws, so they could tear flesh.

Tyrannosaurus

meat-eater's tooth

▷ Tyrannosaurus was the biggest meat-eater. Small meat-eaters fed on other kinds of small animals, but fierce Tyrannosaurus fed on other dinosaurs.

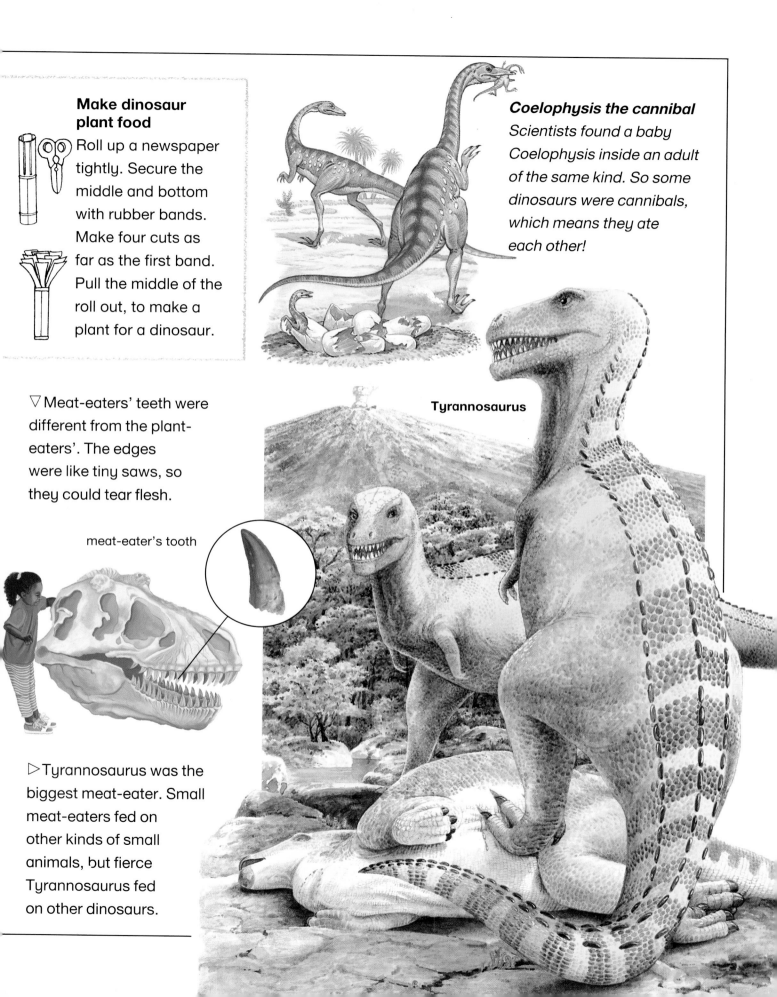

Hunting and defending

Some plant-eaters could move very fast. They could often outrun their enemies. Other dinosaurs moved more slowly and had body weapons. Tough armoured plates, sharp spikes and horns helped to protect them from their enemies.

Meat-eaters were always looking for a tasty meal, so plant-eaters had to be able to escape quickly or fight.

hand

claw

foot

△ Deinonychus had long fingers to grip onto flesh and a terrible slashing claw on its back feet which could rip and tear.

▽ Deinonychus was only the size of a human adult, so it had to hunt in packs to catch larger dinosaurs. The pack would corner the animal, bring it to the ground and kill it.

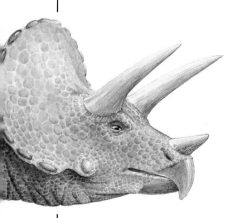

◁ Triceratops had three horns for fighting off a meat-eater. Also a large bony shield protected its neck. Some attackers were put off by such strong protection.

▽ Ankylosaurus had bony armour over its back and head, and a hard club on the end of its tail. So it was able to defend itself.

club

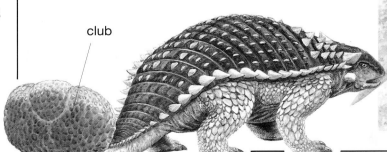

▷ Even the giant Diplodocus needed to defend itself. Diplodocus could lash its long tail like a whip to keep the meat-eaters away.

Make an Ankylosaurus
Cut out a cardboard Ankylosaurus shape, like the one shown here. Cut up an egg carton and glue on the cups. Add screwed up tissue paper and bottletops. Paint it brightly.

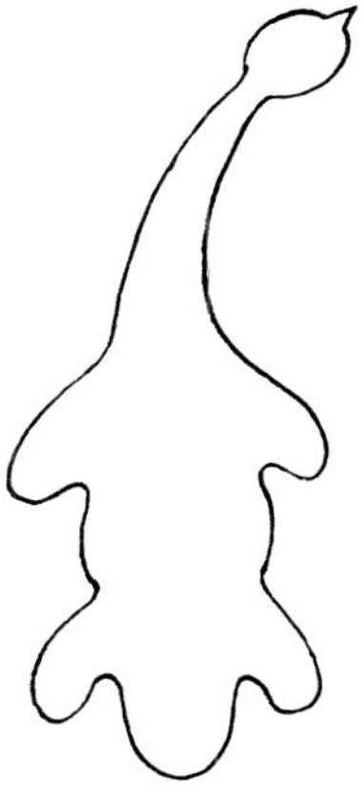

▽ Iguanodon had two sharp thumb spikes. A nasty stab from one of those would often be enough to scare off enemies.

Deinonychus
(**Dine**-o-**nike**-us)

What is evolution?

The Earth is very, very old. The first plants and animals were tiny cells in the sea. Bigger plants and animals slowly developed from these cells. This is called evolution. Dinosaurs first appeared 230 million years ago. They became extinct, which means they died out, 65 million years ago.

the first living things appeared in the sea 3,500 million years ago

the first amphibians lived 395 million years ago

the first reptiles lived on land 310 million years ago

▽ Imagine the age of the Earth as one day and one night on a clock. It is midnight now. Humans appeared at one minute to midnight. Dinosaurs arrived just before eleven.

all the dinosaurs became extinct 65 million years ago

the first humans lived two million years ago

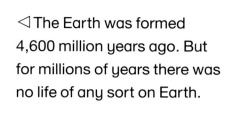

◁ The Earth was formed 4,600 million years ago. But for millions of years there was no life of any sort on Earth.

ERA	STARTED
Archeozoic	4000 million years ago
Proterozoic	2500 million years ago
Palaeozoic	570 million years ago
Mesozoic	245 million years ago
Cenozoic	65 million years ago

the first fish lived in the sea 475 million years ago, when there was no life on land

the first plants grew on land 430 million years ago

the first dinosaurs lived 230 million years ago

the first birds appeared 145 million years ago

today humans share the Earth with many animals and evolution is still going on

Word box
Evolution is how life on Earth has developed from the tiny cells of millions of years ago. **Extinct** means that all of a certain animal or plant group has died out for ever.

Dinosaurs disappear

Dinosaurs roamed the world for 165 million years. This time is called the Mesozoic Era. No dinosaur bones are found from after this time. Dinosaurs became extinct, which means that they died out and disappeared for ever. But why did they disappear?

Triassic period

PALAEOZOIC ERA

△ We divide time into sections, called eras. Dinosaurs lived during the Mesozoic Era. The Mesozoic Era is split into three periods: Triassic, Jurassic and Cretaceous. Different dinosaurs lived in each period, but none lived after the Mesozoic Era.

▽ Not only did the dinosaurs die out. Pterosaurs, Ammonites and the great sea reptiles also disappeared.

victims

▽ A few types of animals survived. Insects, fish, frogs, birds, mammals and some reptiles live today.

survivors

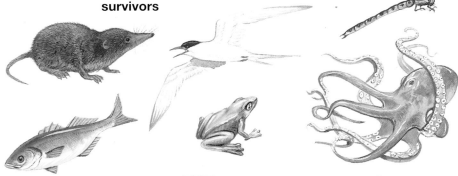

Word box
Mammals are warm-blooded animals with hair or fur. Baby mammals feed on milk from their mother's body.
Ice ages are times, long ago, when ice covered much more of the land than it does today.

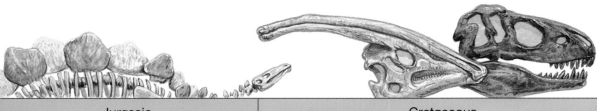

Jurassic period	Cretaceous period	

MESOZOIC ERA

CENOZOIC ERA

Why did they die?

Nobody knows exactly why the dinosaurs died.

▷ Perhaps they were too big. But the smaller ones disappeared as well.

◁ Perhaps dinosaurs were too stupid to survive. But if that were true, why did they survive for so long?

▷ Perhaps new plants poisoned them. But there were other plants to eat.

◁ Maybe mammals ate too many dinosaur eggs. But this would have killed the dinosaurs off earlier.

Some scientists believe dinosaurs were killed when a meteorite hit Earth. This made a huge dust cloud, blocking out the sun. The dinosaurs may have died without the sun's warmth.

Building a dinosaur

Dinosaur bones are taken to a laboratory to be studied. Scientists carefully work on the bones to clean and protect them. This may take years to do. If enough bones are found, a whole dinosaur is put together. This is like fitting together a huge and complicated jigsaw puzzle.

Build a model dinosaur
Draw large outlines of the dinosaur's body and legs onto stiff card, using the shapes shown as a guide. Cut them out and colour in. Cut slits in body and legs, as shown. Put the model together by pushing leg slits into body slits.

△ Scientists remove the protective plaster cases with saws.

△ The bones are cleaned under a microscope.

△ The bones are put on a frame, to make a whole skeleton.

△ A model is made to show what the dinosaur looked like.

▷ Then, the dinosaur is ready for people to come and view it.

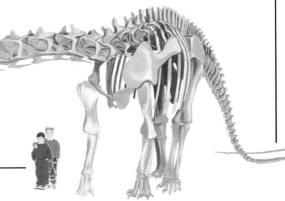

My Body

Body parts

The human body is made up of different parts. At the top is a head, with hair on it. The head is on a neck. Below that is a torso. This is the middle part of the body. We have two arms and two legs that are joined to the torso. Arms and legs are also called limbs. These parts of the body help it to do different things.

Superman
Superman is a story character. He is very strong and can fly faster than any aircraft. He has X-ray vision, which means he can see through anything. He uses his special powers to help others in the world.

Word box
Torso is the main part of the human body, to which the head, arms and legs are attached.
Limbs are the arms and legs of human beings and other animals.

△ Hair protects our head. It helps keep it warm in winter and stops it from burning in the summer sun.

▽ We have feet at the bottom of our legs. Our feet are flat so that we can stand on them and walk upright.

What are you made of?

Most of your body is water. The rest is a mixture of chemicals. The water and chemical mix is arranged in tiny things called cells. Cells make up your skin, muscles, nerves, bones, blood and all the other parts of your body. Cells are so small they can only be seen by using a microscope. Although all the cells have things in common they do not all look the same. There are several hundred different kinds of cells in the body. The smallest cells are red blood cells. They carry food to all the other cells in the body.

▷ Our head is on our neck. The neck bends and turns. This means that our head can move up and down and from side to side.

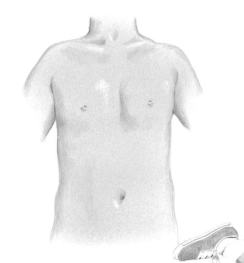

◁ Our neck, arms and legs are attached to our torso. This is the largest part of the body. It can twist, turn and bend in the middle.

▷ We move on our legs. They are long and strong. Legs let us stand upright and walk, run and jump.

▽ Our arms can bend and stretch. We use them to reach for things and use our hands to hold them.

"Simon Says" game

One person is Simon. Simon faces the other players and says, "Simon says pat your head" (or similar). The rest copy. If Simon says, "Pat your toes" without "Simon says" first, the rest stand still. Anyone who moves is out. The last person left is Simon next time.

The skin

Skin covers the whole body. It keeps the parts inside us safe. Skin is tough, but it can also be hurt. It can be burned, cut or bruised. If skin is broken, it will bleed. Skin is not always the same colour. A brown colouring, called melanin, helps protect the skin from sunlight. Black skin has more melanin than white skin.

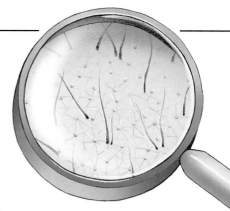

△ When you look at skin under a magnifying glass, it is not smooth. It has bumps on it and small holes. Hairs grow through these holes.

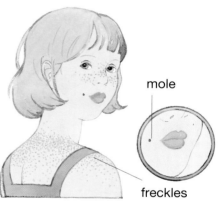

△ Freckles and moles are patches of extra melanin on the skin. Freckles can come and go, but moles stay.

△ Skin may be burned by the sun. It goes red, then peels off. Skin can be protected with sunscreen creams.

▷ Sometimes our skin changes colour. We may go white if we are frightened and red if we are embarrassed.

△ If you fall down, you sometimes break your skin, or graze it. Grazed skin bleeds.

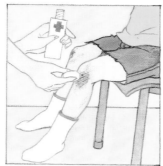

△ The graze can be cleaned with a disinfectant to get rid of dirt and germs.

▽ A bandage keeps the wound clean. The blood dries up and new skin grows.

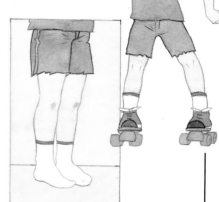

▽ Marks appear on our skin when it is hurt in any way. These marks have different names, depending on what caused them. They look different too.

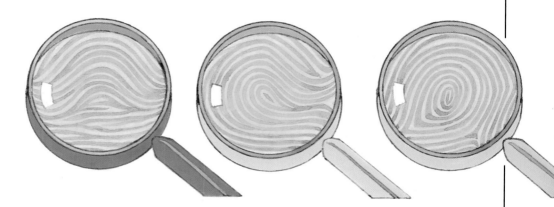

△ Every person in the world has their own special fingerprint pattern.

callus   blister

pinch mark

bruise

Make fingerprints
Lightly rub a thin coating of lipstick onto your fingertip. Press the fingertip on a piece of paper. It will leave a print. Do the same for your friends. Now look at the prints through a magnifying glass and see how different they are.

Hair and nails

We have hair all over our bodies, except for our palms and the soles of our feet. A lot of this hair is too fine to see easily. Hair grows thickest on our heads.

Nails protect our toes and fingertips. Our hair and nails are both made from a substance called keratin.

Rapunzel
(A story by the Brothers Grimm)

A witch shut Rapunzel in a tower. A prince climbed up her long hair to rescue her.

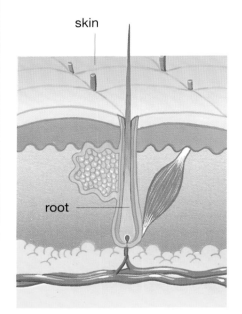 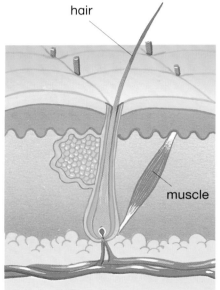

◁ You see only part of the hair. The rest is under the skin and is called the root. When you are cold, a little muscle pulls the hair upright.

◁ Our fingernails and toenails are made of hard keratin. Under the nail, there is soft skin. Under the skin there is bone.

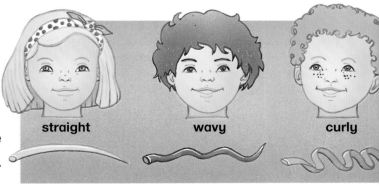

straight · wavy · curly

△ Some hair grows straight, some grows wavy and some grows curly. It comes in lots of different colours too.

Muscles

Our muscles are under our skin. We use muscles whenever we move. Muscles are joined to our bones. They move by becoming shorter or longer. Muscles move every part of the body, not just the bones. Our face muscles move our mouths. Our chest muscles help us to breathe.

△ The muscles in our face help us smile, frown, wink and chew. When we smile, we may use fifteen different muscles.

△ Muscles grow bigger and stronger with exercise and training. Athletes and people who play sports often have strong muscles.

▷ We have more than 650 muscles. There are muscles in every part of our body.

Find the answers

How many muscles do we use when we smile?

What makes muscles grow strong?

Bones and joints

There are over 200 bones in your body. Together, they form the skeleton. Bones support the body and give it shape. They also protect the soft organs inside the body. The places where the bones meet are called joints. Bones are very strong, but they can break.

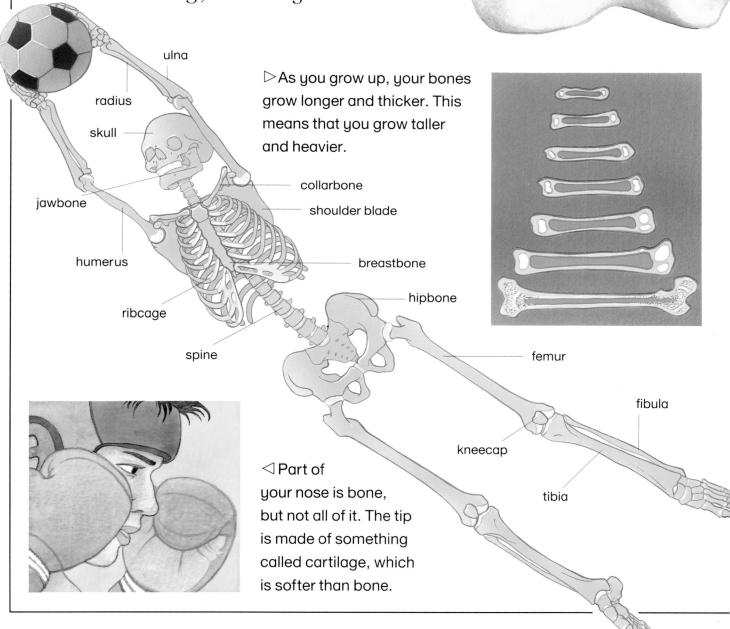

Find the answers

What is the tip of your nose made of?

Name four joints

ulna

radius

skull

jawbone

humerus

ribcage

spine

collarbone

shoulder blade

breastbone

hipbone

▷As you grow up, your bones grow longer and thicker. This means that you grow taller and heavier.

femur

fibula

kneecap

tibia

◁ Part of your nose is bone, but not all of it. The tip is made of something called cartilage, which is softer than bone.

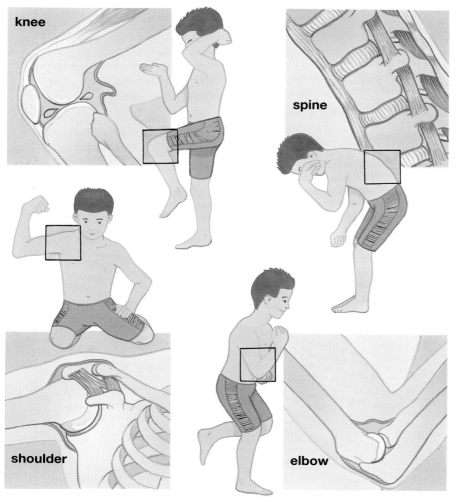

knee

spine

shoulder

elbow

Make a scary skeleton costume

Draw bone shapes, like the ones below, on a large sheet of white paper. Cut them out. Safety pin the bones to a black T-shirt and black leggings. Then put the clothes on. When you lift your arms and legs the skeleton will move.

△ Our knees, spine, shoulders and elbows are some of the joints where bones meet. Some bones fit together, others slide over each other.

△ Bones may break in a fall. A broken bone is called a fracture.

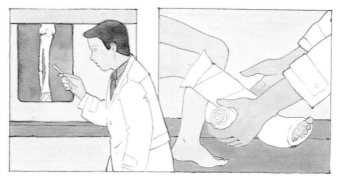

△ A doctor X-rays the bone to see the break.

△ Plaster holds the bone straight while it grows back together again.

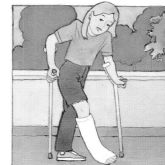

109

Body organs

There are soft parts called organs inside your body. They are protected by the bones and skin. The organs include the brain, lungs, liver, heart, pancreas, kidneys, stomach and intestines. Each of the organs has a special job to do. The brain tells all the other organs what to do. Together, they help the body to work properly.

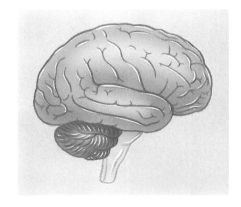

△ The brain is very important because it tells your body how to work. It controls all the other organs.

▷ The brain is in the head. Other organs are in the torso, the main part of the body. They are all different shapes, but they fit together very neatly.

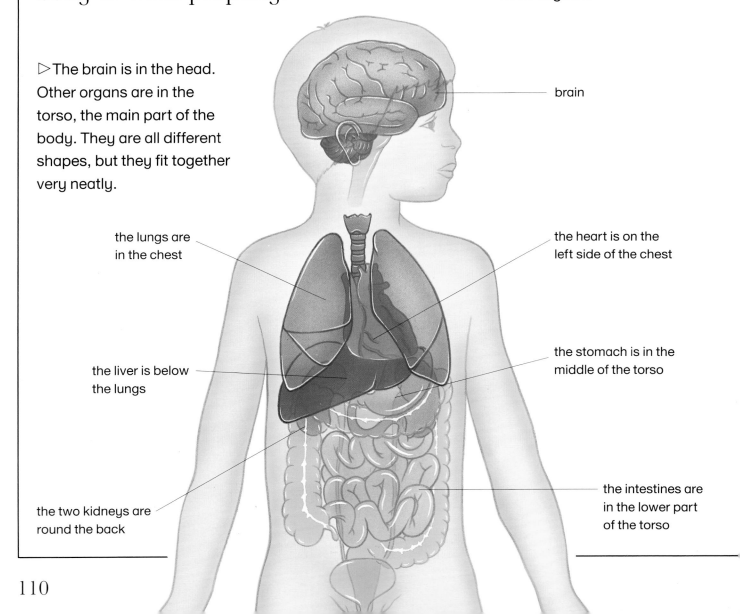

brain

the lungs are in the chest

the heart is on the left side of the chest

the liver is below the lungs

the stomach is in the middle of the torso

the two kidneys are round the back

the intestines are in the lower part of the torso

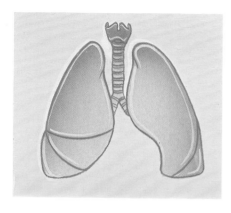

△ We breathe with our lungs. They take air into the body.

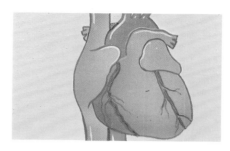

△ The heart pumps blood around the body.

△ The food we eat goes down into the stomach. It turns the food into a pulp before it goes into the intestines.

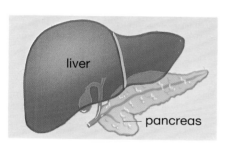

liver

pancreas

△ The liver and pancreas help us to digest our food.

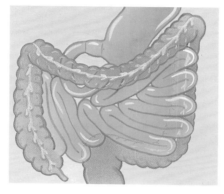

△ The intestines pass liquid food into the blood.

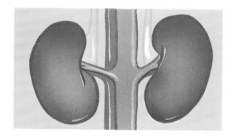

△ Two kidneys help to get rid of the waste from our blood and produce urine from it.

The Wizard of Oz
(A story by L. Frank Baum)

In The Wizard of Oz, *Dorothy meets some characters who have organs missing. Tin Man has no heart and Straw Man has no brain. In this picture from the film, you can see Dorothy and Straw Man on the yellow brick road. They all travel along the yellow brick road in search of the Wizard, who they hope will help them.*

How are we made?

The body is made of lots of tiny living parts called cells. Before we are born we all begin as one cell inside our mother's body. A baby grows in a place called the womb. Genes are parts of the cell that tell it how to grow. Every baby has genes from both the mother's and father's cells.

△ Every baby is made by a man and a woman. They are called its parents.

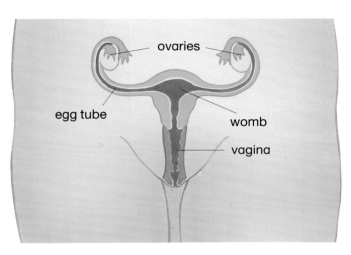

△ These are the organs which a woman has to make a baby. The ovaries produce eggs.

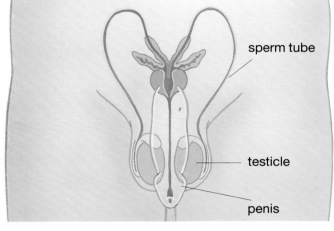

△ These are the organs which a man has to make a baby. The testicles produce sperm.

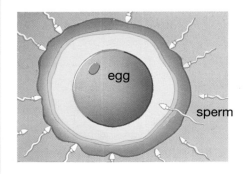

△ A sperm enters an egg. This makes the baby's first cell.

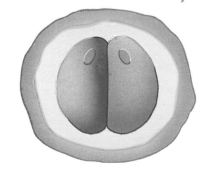

△ The egg splits into two cells. It will then split into four.

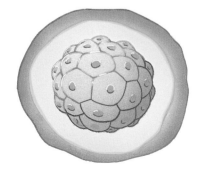

△ It goes on splitting and grows bigger and bigger.

▷A doctor or a special nurse called a midwife checks that the baby is growing properly in its mother's womb. A scanning machine shows the baby inside her.

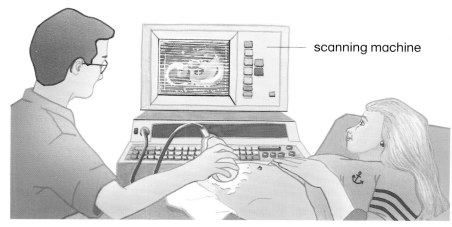

scanning machine

◁Sometimes a mother has two babies from one egg. They are identical twins. Identical twins are two boys or two girls who look just like each other.

▷A mother may also have twins from two eggs. These twins are not identical. The children do not grow up to look alike.

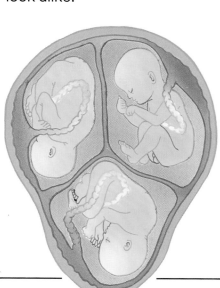

◁Sometimes a mother may have three, four, five or six babies. This is very rare. It is called a multiple birth.

Word box
Cells are tiny living parts that make up our bodies.
Genes are the instructions in cells that decide how living things will develop.
Womb is the place inside the mother where a baby grows until it is born.

Nine months for a baby

The baby grows in a bag of warm liquid in the mother's womb. It gets all the food and oxygen it needs from its mother's body, through a tube called the umbilical cord. After nine months, the baby is born. The mother may give birth in a hospital.

▽ When a baby is about three months old it looks like this. This is a life-size picture.

a sperm enters an egg to make the first cell of the baby

at one month, the baby is no bigger than a pea

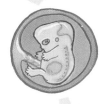
at three months, the baby is about 6 cm long

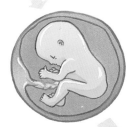
at four months, the baby can move about

at five months, it sucks its thumb

at six months, the baby can hear sounds

at seven months, it opens its eyes and kicks strongly

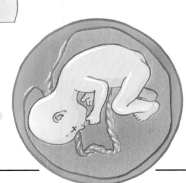

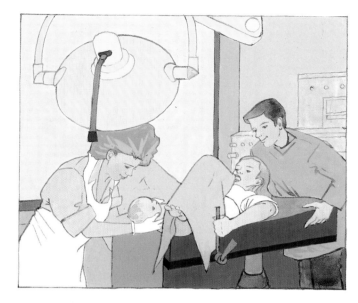

◁ When the baby is ready to be born, the mother may go to hospital to give birth. Her muscles help to push the baby out. Usually the baby comes out head first.

△ The doctor or midwife helps the baby to come out. The baby takes its first breath and cries. It does not need the umbilical cord after it is born, as it can get food and air from outside. So the cord is cut off.

at nine months, it is ready to be born

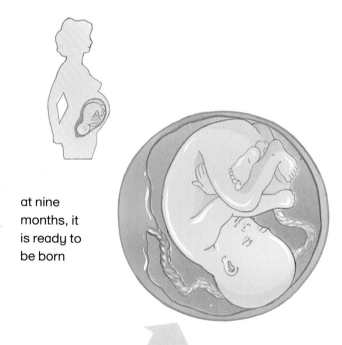

at eight months, it can taste things

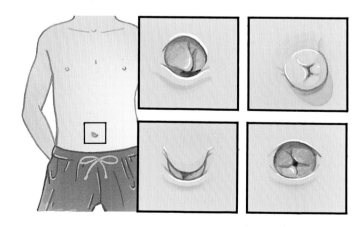

△ When the umbilical cord is cut, it leaves a scar. This becomes our navel, or bellybutton. Bellybuttons can be several different shapes, depending on how the cord was cut.

Seeing

The senses are ways that help us to know what is happening around us. Seeing is a sense. We see with our eyes.

Light comes into our eyes. It sends messages to the brain that then tells us what we see.

Our eyes are protected by eyelids and cleaned by tears.

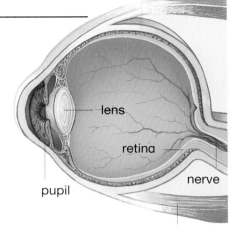

△ The pupil is the black circle in the centre of our eyes. It takes in light. Behind it are the lens, retina and nerves.

▷ The eye has muscles attached to it, so it can move up and down and side to side.

◁ Every time we blink, our eyelids spread tears over our eyes to keep them clean.

◁ In bright light, we need dark glasses to protect our eyes against the glare.

The Emperor's New Clothes
(A story by Hans Andersen)

The Emperor was tricked into wearing no clothes. He was told his new clothes were made out of special cloth that fools could not see. Really, no one could see the clothes.

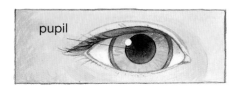
pupil

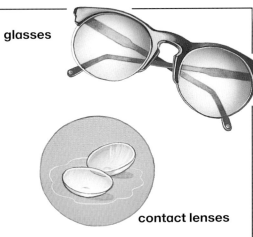
glasses

▷Not everyone can see well. Sometimes we need help to make our sight better. That is why a lot of people wear glasses or contact lenses. These improve the eyesight.

contact lenses

△ When it is dark, our pupils grow larger. They do this to let in more light. This is to help us see better.

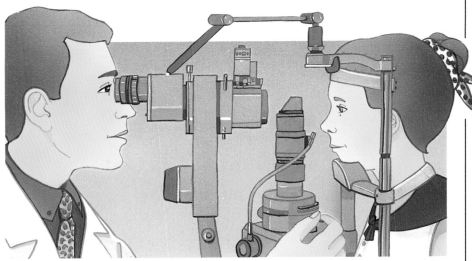

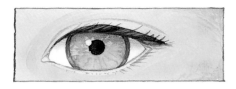

△ In daylight, the light is bright. Our pupils do not need to let in so much light, so they become smaller.

▽ Some people cannot see at all. They are blind. Some blind people have guide dogs to help them find their way.

△ Opticians look after people's eyes. They have special instruments to find out if anything is wrong. They can see through the pupil to the retina at the back of the eye.

Word box
Senses are the way we see, hear, smell, taste and touch the world around us.
Nerves carry messages to and fro between the brain and the different parts of the body.

Smelling

We use our noses to breathe and to smell. Smells float in the air. We smell things when we take in air through our noses. Smells are invisible, but our noses send messages to the brain, which tells us what they are.

Smells come from many different things around us. Some smells are nice, some are not. Our sense of smell also helps our sense of taste.

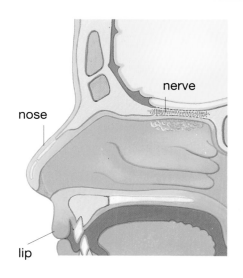

△ When a smell reaches the back of our nose, nerves tell the brain about it.

◁ There are some special doctors who look after people's noses, ears and throats only.

◁ If our nose is blocked and we cannot smell things, it is hard to taste them.

Can you find?

1 cheese
2 flower
3 soap
4 car exhaust fumes
5 scent

Find the answers

What do we use the nose for?

Why can you not see smells?

Tasting

We taste things with our tongues. There are thousands of little bumps all over the tongue called taste buds. Inside them are nerves that send messages to the brain about what we are eating. There are four main types of taste: sweet, salty, bitter and sour. Each is tasted by different parts of the tongue and mouth. The tongue is also able to feel heat, cold and pain.

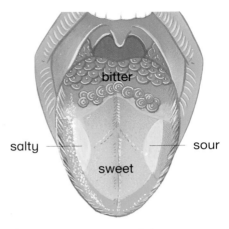

△ Different parts of the tongue are good at picking up different tastes. There are taste buds at the front, back and sides of the tongue.

△ The front of the tongue tastes sweet things mainly.

△ The sides taste salty things.

△ The sides also taste sour things.

△ The back tastes bitter things mainly.

Try tasting without smelling

Put water in four cups. Add salt to one, lemon juice to another and sugar to another. Leave the fourth. Ask a friend to hold their nose and taste them. See if they can tell the difference. Without smell, they should all taste the same.

Hearing

We hear sounds all the time. They tell us about the world around us. Sounds are vibrations in the air. We cannot see them. We hear sounds through our ears.

We can only see a part of the ear, the part that is outside the head. The rest of the ear is inside the head.

Some people cannot hear very well. People who cannot hear well are deaf.

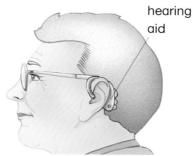

△ Sounds make the eardrum move. This makes three tiny bones move. A nerve carries the message to the brain.

▽ There are all sorts of different sounds around us. Builders need to wear earmuffs to protect their ears from very loud sounds.

◁ A hearing aid helps people who cannot hear very well. It is a small machine which goes into the ear and makes sounds louder.

Helen Keller

Helen Keller could not hear, speak or see. She learnt to listen to people by placing her fingers on their lips and throat and feeling the vibrations that their voice made.

Touching

When we touch things, we can feel them. We can feel heat, cold, pain, softness, hardness and sharpness. Nerves just under the surface of the skin help us to feel things. They send messages to the brain about what we touch. We can feel best with the tips of our fingers because that is the place where we have the most nerves.

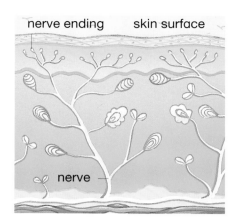

△ Tiny nerves in the skin send the brain messages about the things we touch. Nerves end just under the skin surface.

△ When we hold a drink of hot cocoa we can feel the heat through the cup.

▽ This blind person can read and write Braille, by using her sense of touch.

△ Pianists use their sense of touch to control sound. They can play softly or loudly depending on the pressure.

△ If we touch a thorn we feel a sharp prick on our fingers.

Feely game

Put some objects in a bag. They should all feel different. Ask your friends to put their hands in the bag and feel them. They must guess what the objects are by touch alone.

Breathing

We need air that contains oxygen to stay alive. The lungs take oxygen from the air we inhale, or breathe in. They also exhale, or breathe out, used air. Blood takes the oxygen from the lungs and carries it to the rest of the body.

The lungs work very hard. Every day we take about 23,000 breaths!

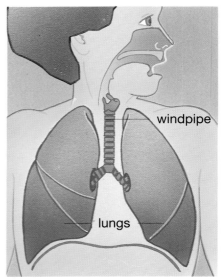

△ When you inhale, or breathe in, air goes down the windpipe into the lungs. Blood in the lungs collects oxygen and takes it around the body.

△ Exercising in fresh mountain air is good for us. The air is cleaner than in the cities where there are often fumes from traffic and factories.

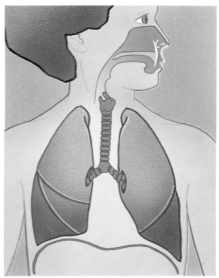

△ Blood also carries used air back to the lungs. When you exhale, or breathe out, your lungs push used air back out through your nose or mouth.

Word box
Inhale is what we do when we breathe in. The lungs become bigger and the air rushes in.
Exhale is what we do when we breathe out. The lungs become smaller, pushing the air out again.

The Three Little Pigs
(An English folk tale)

Three little pigs each built a home. The first built a house of straw. The second built one of twigs. The third used bricks. A wicked wolf blew down the first two houses. But his lungs and breath were not strong enough to blow down the brick house.

◁ It is impossible to stay underwater without a snorkel or air tank, because there is no air to breathe. Most of us need to breathe at least 20 times a minute.

Blow football game
Make two goal posts with straws, using plasticine as shown. Place one at each end of a table. Make a scrunched-up paper ball. Each player chooses a home goal. The idea is to blow the ball into the other player's goal. Each goal scored earns one point. Play for five minutes. The winner is the one with the most points.

△ People who have asthma may use an inhaler to help them to breathe. Their air passages are narrower than usual. This causes noisy breathing or wheezing. The inhaler puffs or squirts a drug which makes their air passages wider, so they can breathe more easily.

123

Blood supply

Blood flows around the body through thin tubes called veins and arteries. It carries oxygen from the air we breathe in and goodness from food that we eat. It also helps to fight germs. The heart is a hollow muscle that pumps blood each time it beats. It must be strong enough to send blood to every cell in the body.

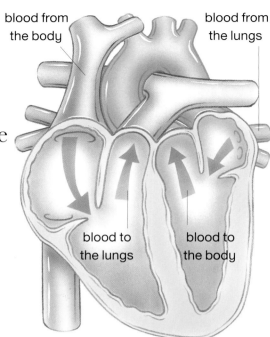

blood from the body

blood from the lungs

blood to the lungs

blood to the body

△ One side of the heart receives blood from the body and sends it to the lungs to collect oxygen. The other side receives blood carrying oxygen back from the lungs. This is then pumped around the body.

heart

artery

vein

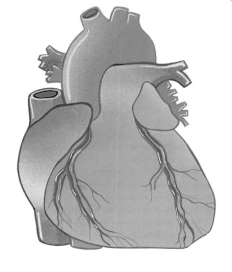

◁ The heart beats about 70 times each minute.

Make a stethoscope

A doctor uses a stethoscope to listen to patients' heartbeats. To make your own stethoscope, push a piece of tubing over the end of a funnel, as shown. Hold the funnel to your patient's chest and put the tubing near your ear. You will be able to hear their heartbeat.

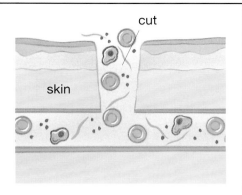

cut

skin

△ When you cut yourself, the white cells attack any germs that get in and platelets rush to plug the cut blood vessels.

▷ Blood contains red cells, white cells and platelets in a liquid called plasma. Red cells carry oxygen and white cells help fight germs. Platelets help the blood to clot.

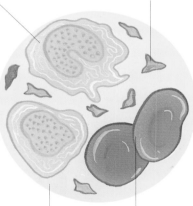

white cell

platelet

plasma

red cell

blood clot   scab

skin

△ A sticky clot is formed. This hardens into a scab that protects the wound.

healed cut

skin

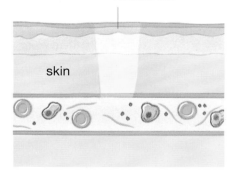

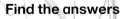

Find the answers

What does a scab do?

How many times does the heart beat a minute?

△ As the wound heals, new skin grows underneath. This is pink when the scab drops off.

The nervous system

Nerves all through our bodies take messages from our senses to the brain. This is called the nervous system. The brain is the most important part of the body because it tells it how to work. It helps us to feel things and to think, learn and remember. Part of the brain also helps us to balance.

▽ Your brain helps you to think and concentrate.

▽ Your brain helps you to move at different speeds.

▽ It helps you to learn how to swim.

▽ It helps you to keep your balance.

▽ It helps you to walk and to talk.

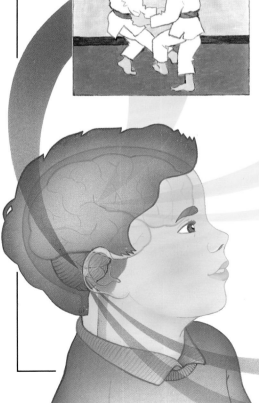

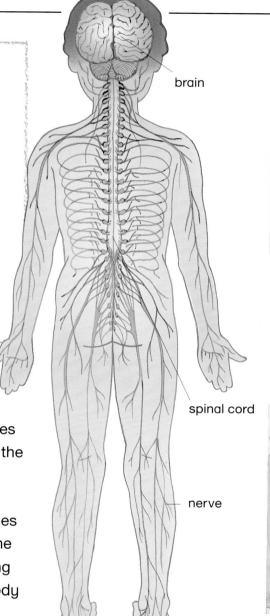

Play the memory game
Ask a friend to put ten objects on a tray. There could be a watch, a cup, a pen, a coin, a book and so on. Look at the tray for one minute, then cover it up. Write down all the things you saw. Can you remember every single one?

brain

spinal cord

nerve

▷ Messages from our senses pass through the nerves to the spinal cord. This is a thick bundle of nerves down the middle of our backs. It carries signals to the brain. Then the brain sends messages along other nerves that tell the body what to do.

△ Sometimes the nervous system reacts very quickly. This happens when you are in danger of hurting yourself.

△ When you touch something sharp, your hand will jerk away. You do not have to think about it. This is called a reflex action.

◁ When you learn something, the brain stores it so that you can remember it another time. This is called memory.

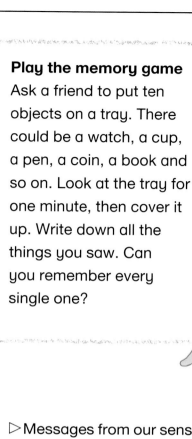

Teeth

We bite into food and chew it with our teeth so it is easier to swallow. Our teeth are different shapes and they do different things. Teeth are fixed into our jaws, but they can come loose. Children lose their first teeth and grow another, larger set. If we do not brush our teeth, they will rot, or decay.

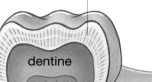
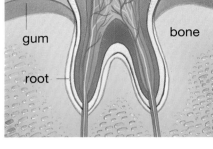

enamel
dentine
pulp
gum
bone
root

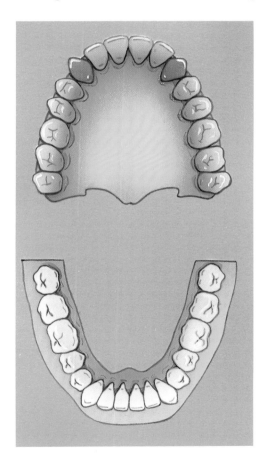

△ The sharp incisors at the front are for cutting food. Pointed canines at the sides tear it. Big molars at the back crush it.

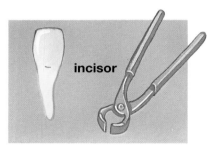

incisor

△ Incisors cut like pliers.

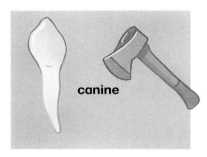

canine

△ Canines cut like an axe.

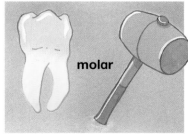

molar

△ Molars crush like a hammer.

△ The outside of the tooth is a hard layer of enamel. This covers the dentine. Inside this is the pulp. Roots hold the tooth in place in the jawbone.

The Tooth Fairy
Some people say that if you lose a tooth, you should put it under your pillow. Then the Tooth Fairy will come and take it away. Sometimes the Tooth Fairy leaves money in exchange for the tooth.

▷When we are about six years old, our first teeth become loose and fall out. Larger teeth grow underneath.

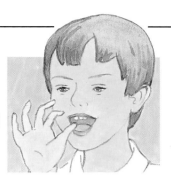

◁The dentist looks after our teeth. If he finds a decaying tooth, he removes the decay and fills the hole with hard paste.

Make an eggshell decay
Ask an adult to hard boil an egg. Put it in a cup of malt vinegar. Leave it for a day, then see how much of the shell has been eaten away by the vinegar. This is what fizzy drinks and sweets do to your teeth.

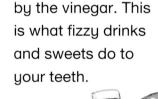

△Some people wear a brace or a plate to make crooked teeth straight.

△Brush your teeth for three minutes.

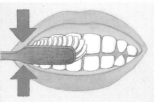

△Brush up and down the front of your teeth.

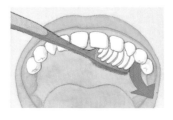

△Then brush up and down the back.

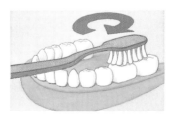

△Always brush with a circular movement.

Eating for energy

We eat food because it gives our bodies energy. People eat many different kinds of food, but our bodies use everything in the same way. When you swallow food, it moves down a tube into the stomach and then into the intestines. On the way, the goodness is taken out of the food. This is called digestion.

The Magic Porridge Pot
(A story by the Brothers Grimm)

A lady gave a tired, hungry girl a magic pot and told her magic words to make the pot cook delicious, nourishing porridge. But when the girl's mother used the magic pot she forgot how to stop it. The porridge flooded the whole village! When the girl stopped the pot, they had to eat their way into their home!

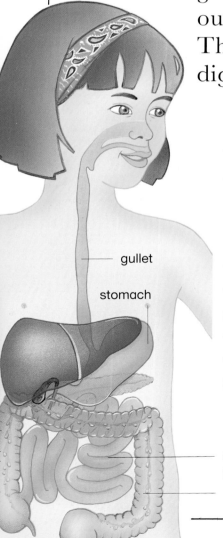

gullet

stomach

small intestine

large intestine

◁ Food goes down the gullet to the stomach, which mashes it up. Then it is squeezed along the intestines. It passes through the intestine walls into the blood. Solid fibre passes through as waste when all the goodness has been taken out.

△ In different parts of the world, people eat different types of food. All of it gives the body the energy it needs to live.

Science

What is science?

Science is about finding out. It helps us make sense of our world. Science begins with observation. This means looking at things very carefully. Scientists work in different ways and study many subjects, such as biology, astronomy, medicine, geology and chemistry. Much has been discovered through science, but there is a lot left to find out about our world.

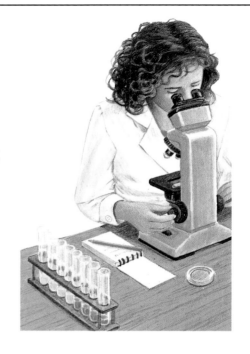

△ Scientists often use special tools, such as microscopes, to help them observe.

The senses
Observation does not mean using just our eyes, but all our senses to find out things.

touching a tree to see if it is smooth or rough

smelling an egg to see if it is bad

tasting a lemon to find out if it is sweet or sour

looking in a book to find answers to questions

listening for high and low sounds

△ We can all be scientists. These children are studying the wildlife in a pond.

▷This scientist is a marine biologist. She is studying sea life.

△Astronomers use telescopes to study the stars. They find out about the Universe.

▽ Doctors study medicine. They do experiments, or tests, to find out if new drugs can fight diseases.

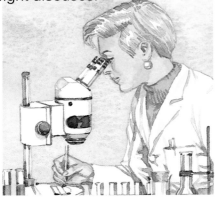

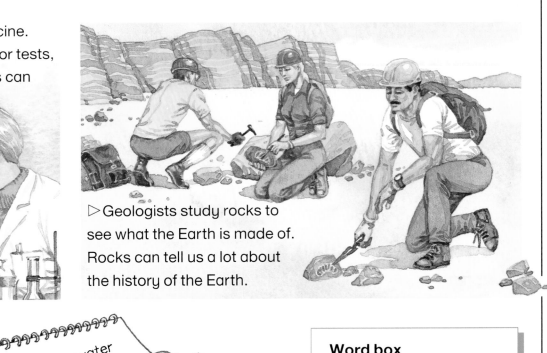

▷Geologists study rocks to see what the Earth is made of. Rocks can tell us a lot about the history of the Earth.

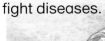

H_2O=water

▷Chemists use special symbols, or signs, to study chemistry. Doctors and other scientists use these symbols, too.

Word box
Observation is how we find out about the world around us. We need to use our senses to do this. **Experiments** are the tests scientists carry out to see if their ideas are correct.

Materials and structures

The things around us are made from different materials, such as wood, plastic and metal. Different materials do different jobs. A sponge soaks up water. A metal saucepan is strong and can stand up to heat.

The way something is put together is called its structure. Structure can also help to make things strong.

△ These objects are made from many materials. Some are strong, some are soft and others stand up to heat.

△ This lighthouse is made from materials that can stand up to stormy weather.

△ The glass in a greenhouse lets the sun's rays pass through and traps heat, so the plants stay warm.

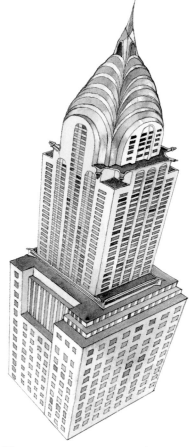

△ Skyscrapers are made from strong, hard materials that will last a long time.

Word box
Materials are used to make things. Materials are carefully chosen to suit the jobs they have to do.
Structures are the ways materials are put together to make them stronger.

△ This bridge has stood for years. The stone it is made from is a strong material.

Build a roof

Arrange two cereal packets alongside each other. These are your walls. Open a hardback book in the middle and try to balance it on the walls to make a roof. You will find that the weight of the roof pushes the two walls apart. Now lay two rulers across the cereal packets, as shown. Does the book balance now?

△ The shape of a structure is important. Cylinders look like tubes. They are very strong. A tree's cylinder-shaped trunk supports its heavy branches.

△ Stone columns on buildings are cylinder-shaped. They are able to hold up a lot of weight, such as roofs.

◁ Triangles are strong because no one side can bend away from the other two. The Eiffel Tower is made of many triangles.

▽ Spiders spin strong webs. Can you see the triangles in this web?

Solids, liquids and gases

All materials are either solids, liquids or gases. Solids keep their shape and can be hard or soft. Liquids take the shape of their container. If we pour a liquid, it will run. Gases will not even stay in their container. If they escape, they spread out all over the room.

△ Can you pick out the solids, gases and liquids in this picture?

Icarus
(A Greek myth)

Icarus and his father were imprisoned on the island of Crete. They escaped by making wings of feathers held together with wax. Icarus' father warned him not to fly too near the Sun. But Icarus ignored him. The Sun melted the wax, and Icarus fell.

△ Some materials can turn from solid to liquid to gas. Water from a tap is liquid.

△ If we freeze water, it becomes a solid called ice. Ice melts back into water.

△ If we heat water enough, it becomes a gas called steam. This change is called boiling.

△ If we let steam cool, it turns back into a liquid. This change is called condensation.

△ As wax gets hot, it melts and goes runny. When it cools it becomes solid. Wax can change again and again.

▷ Many materials change when they are heated or cooled. Lava comes out of a volcano as a liquid. As lava cools, it turns into solid rock.

lava

◁ Some things change when they are heated, but cannot change back. A fried egg cannot go back to being raw.

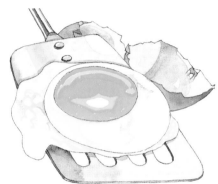

▽ Milk left for a long time goes lumpy and smelly. You cannot undo this change.

Make an ice pop freezer
Put about 20 ice cubes in a bowl. Push a liquid ice pop into bowl and cover with ice. Sprinkle a tablespoon of salt over ice so ice melts. A mixture of salt and ice is colder than ice on its own. After 15 minutes the ice pop will be solid.

▽ A baked cake cannot go back to being the runny mixture it was before it was cooked.

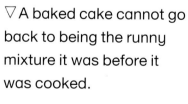

137

Energy

Energy is all around us. We cannot see it, but we can see, hear and feel its effects. When we watch the television, listen to the radio or feel a room warm up, energy is being used.

Energy does not disappear, it changes from one kind to another. Petrol has energy stored in it. When it is used in a car, petrol burns and gives out heat energy. As it makes the car go, the heat energy is turned into movement energy.

Make a windmill

Cut slits in a square of thin card, 24cm by 24cm. Make holes in middle and corners, as shown. Fold corners into middle and line up holes. Thread a pin through. Thread a bead on. Push pin through a strong plastic straw, a bead and a piece of cork. Blow windmill to spin it.

△A sailing boat uses wind energy. This wind energy is caught in the boat's sails and pushes the boat forward.

◁ People and animals turn energy from the food they eat into movement energy.

△ Hairdryers work by turning electrical energy into heat and movement energy.

△ All living things get their energy from the sun.

△ Grass uses sunlight to make food. Cows eat the grass.

◁ Cows use energy from the grass to make milk.

◁ This energy helps us to lead an active life.

◁ We drink the milk, that contains energy.

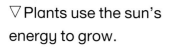

▽ Plants use the sun's energy to grow.

▷ Cars use the petrol to make them go.

◁ Today we drill for oil and turn it into other fuels, such as petrol.

▷ When these plants died, their remains were buried and squashed. Slowly, over millions of years, the dead plants turned into oil.

Word box
Energy is the ability to do work. Everything needs energy to move, work, breathe or grow.
Fuel is stored energy. It is burned to release heat energy to power machines.

139

Heat energy

When you hold a mug of hot cocoa, it warms your hands up. Holding a snowball makes your hands go very cold. This is because hot things pass their heat to their surroundings and lose some heat themselves. Heat always moves from a warmer place to a colder one. Heat energy moves through radiation, conduction or convection.

△ Conduction heats food in a pan. The heat from the cooker moves to the pan, and from the pan it moves to the food.

▽ The sun gives off rays of heat which warm up Earth. This is called radiation.

△ Heat from hot drinks warm up your hands by conduction.

▷ Animals, such as reptiles, use radiation. The sun's rays warm their bodies up. After basking in the sun, this lizard will be warm enough to move around and search for food.

△ Heat from your hands is lost through conduction when you hold a snowball.

▽ This room is being heated by convection. Air near the radiator becomes warm. This warm air rises and is replaced by cooler air, which in turn is heated itself.

Conduction experiment
Some materials conduct heat better than others. To test this, put a wooden spoon, a plastic spoon and a metal spoon into a jug of warm water. Leave for two minutes. Feel the handles. The one that is the warmest conducts heat the best.

▷ Convection is important in heating homes. The warmest place is usually at the top because warm air rises.

▷ The middle of the house is warm, but not as warm as upstairs. The bottom of the house is coolest because cold air sinks. In old houses, the basement was often used as a store for keeping things cool.

Floating and sinking

An object floats on water because of balancing forces. As the weight of an object pulls it down, the water pushes it up. If an object is light for its size, the push of the water balances its weight and the object floats.

The shape of an object is also very important. It allows some heavy metal objects, such as ships, to float. This is because they push aside more water than they weigh themselves.

Find the answers

Do wooden spoons float?

What can we use to keep us afloat when swimming?

some objects float on top of the water's surface

some objects float almost completely under the water

some objects sink to the bottom

△ Some objects float on top of water, others sink to the bottom. Some float near the surface, just under the water.

Make a catamaran

A catamaran is a boat with two hulls. Ask an adult to cut a washing-up liquid bottle in half for hulls. Use waterproof tape to attach thin strips of balsa wood across the hulls, to hold them together.

Float your catamaran in water. How many objects can you put into your catamaran before it sinks?

▽ Air-filled armbands help you float. Air is lighter than water. Objects with lots of air trapped inside them float well.

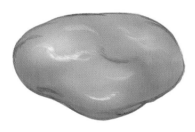

△ A lump of plasticine sinks because it weighs more than the water pushing it up.

▽ The shape of a ship helps it float. This is because it has a lot of air inside it, so is light for its very large size. It pushes aside more water than it weighs itself.

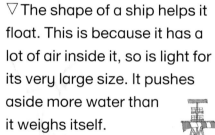

△ If the plasticine is made into a boat, the water has a wider shape to push up. It floats because the plasticine is now lighter for its size.

Light and colour

Sunlight is a kind of energy which comes from the Sun. It travels through Space as light waves. Sunlight seems to be colourless or white. But really it is made up of several colours mixed together.

▽ You can see the colours of sunlight in a rainbow. Light passing through raindrops is split up into red, orange, yellow, green, blue, indigo and violet.

▽ Things are different colours. This is because they soak up some of the colours from light and let the others bounce off them.

△ Transparent materials, such as glass, let nearly all light through.

△ Translucent materials, such as plastic, let some light through.

△ Opaque materials, such as wrapping paper, do not let any light through.

◁ A tomato soaks up all colours except red, which bounces back off it, into our eyes. So we see a red tomato.

Make a rainbow

You can split up light into different colours. On a sunny day, fill a tub with water and put it by a window. Rest a flat mirror against one side of the tub. Angle the mirror to catch the sunlight until a rainbow appears on the ceiling. You could use plasticine to hold the mirror in place once you have made the rainbow.

△ Sunlight travels through Space very quickly. Nothing travels faster than light.

△ At night there is only starlight and moonlight. Long ago, people used fire for light.

△ Later, people used wax candles and oil lamps. Now we mainly use electricity.

Rain's son, the Rainbow
(An Australian folk tale)

Rainbow was Rain's son. He only came out to stop his father from falling from the sky. People had to chase Rainbow away to allow Rain to fall, otherwise there would be a drought.

Word box
Transparent materials let most light pass through.
Translucent materials only let some light through.
Opaque materials do not let any light through.

145

Shadows

Light waves travel in straight lines. They cannot bend around things. If something gets in the way of a light wave, it blocks the light and casts a shadow. The Earth spins as it goes around the Sun. This makes outdoor shadows point in different directions and change length at different times of the day.

Find the answers

When is your shadow longest?

When is the Sun high in the sky?

◁ Your shadow is always longer in the early morning and late afternoon.

▷ At midday, or noon, the Sun is high in the sky, and your shadow is very short.

dog

rabbit

giraffe

bird

Make shadow shapes
In a darkened room, ask a friend to shine a torch onto a wall beside you. Make sure your hands are in between the light rays and the wall. By holding your hands as shown here, you can cast different animal-shaped shadows.

Reflections

When light hits any smooth, shiny surface, it bounces back making a reflection. When you look into a mirror, light bounces off your body, then off the mirror back at you, so you can see your reflection.

The light from the Sun bounces off the Moon, giving us moonlight.

▷ Lots of shiny surfaces reflect light. This boy can see his reflection in an empty saucepan. Can you see yourself in any objects at home?

△ Mirrors are made of a sheet of glass in front of a thin piece of shiny metal.

△ Moonlight is light reflected from the Sun. It is sometimes reflected again in the shiny surface of water.

The Rain Puddle
(A story by Adelaide Holl)

The farmyard animals see their own reflections in a rain puddle and think there are other animals drowning in it. When the sun comes out and dries up the puddle, they foolishly think the reflected animals have been saved.

Sound

Every noise you hear is made by something vibrating, or moving backwards and forwards very quickly.

Sound travels in waves. Sound waves need to have something to move through. They can travel through solids, liquids or gases.

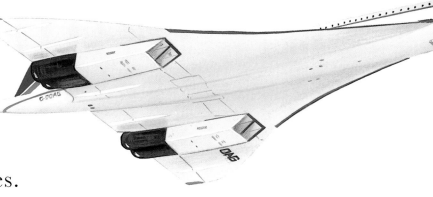

△ Sound travels through the air at about 1,224 kilometres an hour. Concorde is supersonic, it can travel faster than sound.

▽ When someone speaks to you, vibrations pass through their mouth into the air, making the air vibrate. The vibrations travel to your ear in sound waves and you hear them as sound.

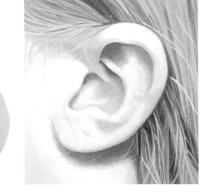

sound waves

Seeing sounds

You cannot see sound waves, but you can see their effects. Make a drum by stretching foil tightly over a bowl. Attach with a rubber band. Put some grains of uncooked rice on the drum. Then bang on the lid of a tin. The sound waves will make the rice bounce.

▽ Lightning and thunder happen at the same time, but we see lightning before we hear thunder. This is because sound travels more slowly than light.

△ Sound travels faster and further through water than air. Whales sing to each other. They can hear each other's songs from up to 100 kilometres away.

△ You can hear sound that has travelled through a solid by putting your ear to a table, and asking a friend to bang a saucepan at the other end.

Word box
Vibrations are fast, regular backwards and forwards movements in solids, liquids and gases.
Sound waves are produced by vibrations. They carry sounds at different speeds through solids, liquids and gases.

Electricity

There are two types of electricity. They are static electricity and current electricity. Current electricity can flow along wires. This means that it can travel from a battery or a power station to where it is needed. Current electricity is very important in our everyday world. Just think of all the things that stop working if there is a power cut!

△ If you comb your hair quickly, it will become charged with static electricity.

Never play with, or go near, current electricity. It could kill you.

▷ These machines work by using current electricity. Without them, our lives would be very different, and much more difficult.

Word box
Power stations burn fuel to make current electricity for use at home and work.
Batteries make current electricity from chemicals stored inside them.

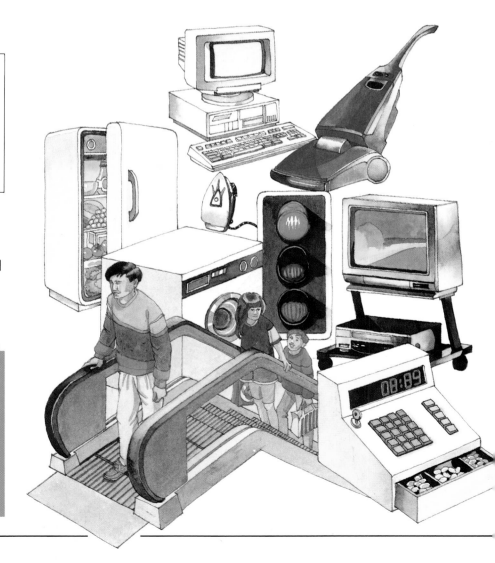

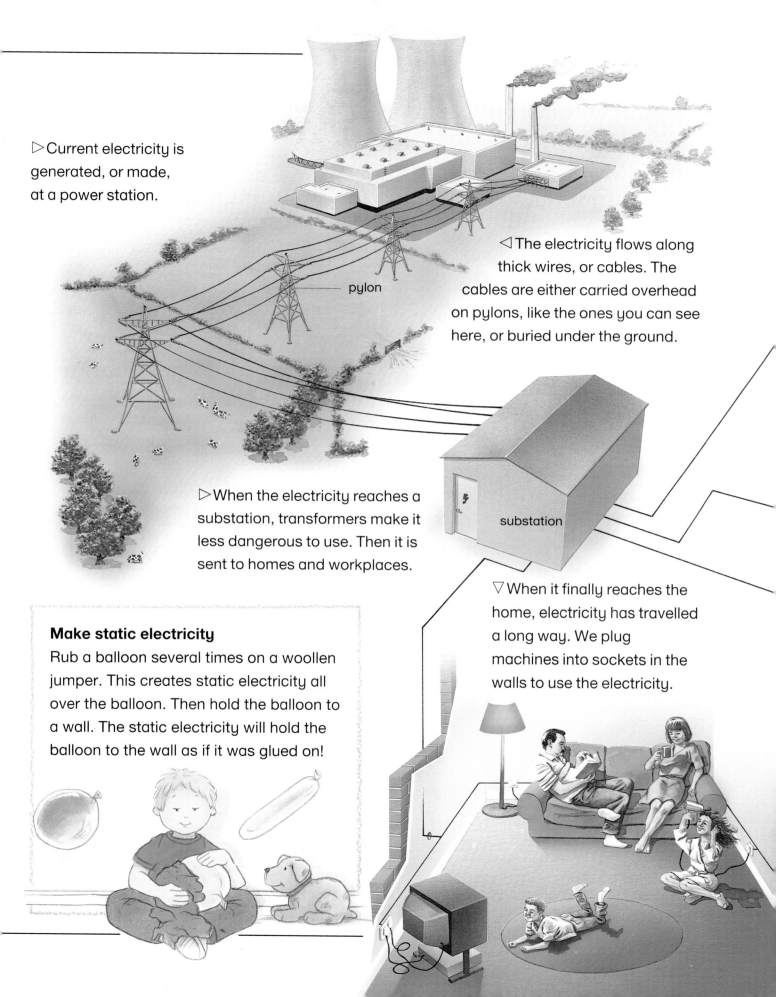

▷ Current electricity is generated, or made, at a power station.

◁ The electricity flows along thick wires, or cables. The cables are either carried overhead on pylons, like the ones you can see here, or buried under the ground.

pylon

▷ When the electricity reaches a substation, transformers make it less dangerous to use. Then it is sent to homes and workplaces.

substation

▽ When it finally reaches the home, electricity has travelled a long way. We plug machines into sockets in the walls to use the electricity.

Make static electricity
Rub a balloon several times on a woollen jumper. This creates static electricity all over the balloon. Then hold the balloon to a wall. The static electricity will hold the balloon to the wall as if it was glued on!

Magnets

A magnet attracts, or pulls, some materials towards it. This is called magnetism and the materials are magnetic. Not everything is magnetic, so there are some things that you cannot pick up with a magnet.

   Every magnet has a north pole and a south pole. These poles are at the ends of a magnet. The north pole of one magnet attracts the south pole of another magnet. Two north poles or two south poles repel, or push apart.

△ If you put the north pole of one magnet near the south pole of another, they are attracted and pull together.

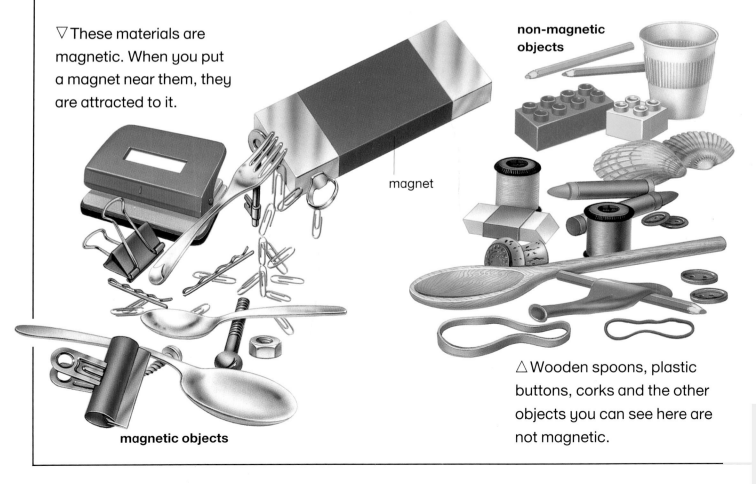

▽ These materials are magnetic. When you put a magnet near them, they are attracted to it.

magnet

non-magnetic objects

magnetic objects

△ Wooden spoons, plastic buttons, corks and the other objects you can see here are not magnetic.

▷Compasses are used to help people find their way. The needle in a compass is a magnet. As the Earth is magnetic, the north-seeking pole of the compass turns to the North Pole of the Earth.

△ The Earth itself is magnetic.

▷Magnets come in all sorts of shapes and sizes. This enormous magnet works in a breakers yard. The magnet picks up and moves huge pieces of scrap metal. It would be difficult to pick up this car without it!

Make a magnetic theatre
Cut slits in four short cardboard tubes. Splay out ends and glue to the bottom corners of a thin cardboard box. Decorate to look like a theatre. Add old material for curtains. Draw characters on thin card. Cut out, leaving a tab, as shown. Fold back tabs and tape on paperclips. Tape strong magnets to sticks. To move the characters, move one magnet under each character.

Backwards and forwards

Things move when something pushes or pulls them. These pushes and pulls are called forces. A force can make something start to move, speed up, slow down, change direction or stop moving. Every force has another force that pushes in the opposite direction.

△ All these children are using forces to make things move.

◁ Three children cannot make the see-saw work. This is because the force pushing down on one end is bigger than the force pushing down on the other end. So, one child is getting off.

Word box
Forces can make things move. Pushes and pulls are forces.
Pendulum is any weight that hangs from a fixed point and swings freely.

△ Two children make the see-saw work. The forces pushing on each end are the same.

154

Make a pendulum

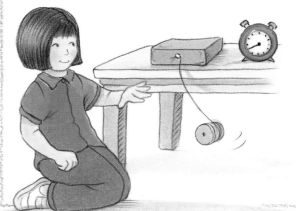

Tie a piece of string around a cotton reel. Attach the loose end of string to a soft block of wood, using a drawing pin, as shown. Fix the block of wood to the edge of an old table with plasticine. Push or pull your pendulum to make it swing. Use a stop clock to see how many swings it makes in 30 seconds. Try making the string longer and count the number of swings again. Are there more or less?

Can you find?

1 push	4 pull
2 pull	5 push
3 push	6 pull

▷When this canoeist pulls the paddle back, he pushes the canoe forwards.

Gravity and weight

The Earth pulls everything towards its centre, including us! This force is called gravity. It is the reason why things always fall down and not up. The Earth's gravity pulls on the Moon too, which keeps it circling around the Earth.

The weight of an object depends on gravity. We call the pull of the Earth's gravity on an object its weight.

△ Apples fall down from trees because gravity pulls them towards the Earth.

▷ You can throw a ball up into the air, but it will always fall back to the ground.

◁ When scales measure your weight, they are measuring the pull of Earth's gravity on your body.

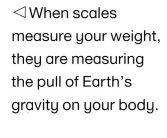

▷ In a spaceship far from the Earth, there is so little gravity that things just float around. Astronauts have to tie themselves down, if they do not want to float about.

Index

This index will help you to find out where you can read information about a subject. It is in alphabetical order.

A

abdomen 66
acorns 35, 75
Africa 31, 36
air 26–27, 122, 143
alligators 87
America 30
ammonites 98
amphibians 55, 62–63
animals 50–51, 54–57,60, 96
Antarctica 30, 32, 45
antennae 66, 67
ants 40, 67
aphids 67
Arctic 32, 33, 45, 46
arms 102, 103
arteries 124
Asia 31
asthma 123
astronomers 133
atmosphere 19
Australia 31, 35, 37
autumn 44, 79
Ayers Rock 31

B

babies 112–115
backbones 54, 55
bats 56
batteries 150
beans 77
bears 33, 34, 56
Beaufort scale 27
bees 73
beetles 66
belly button 115
berries 74, 75
Big Bang 6
birds 26, 55, 58–59, 76, 92, 97

birth 115
blindness 117, 121
blisters 105
blood 122, 124–125
body 102–130
boiling 136
bones 108–109
Braille 121
brain 110, 126–127
breastbone 108
breathing 118, 122–123
bruises 105
bugs 67
buildings 134–135
buntings 33
butterflies 40, 67, 68

C

cactus plants 39, 79
calluses 105
camels 39
camouflage 84, 87
canines 128
carnivores 56, 92, 93
carpels 72, 73, 74
cartilage 108
caterpillars 68
cells 96, 112, 113, 125
chamois 23
chemists 133
chipmunks 34
chlorophyll 70, 71
chrysalis 68
claws 59, 83, 94
climate 30, 32–40
clouds 24, 28–29
collarbone 108
colour 84, 87, 144–145
comets 15
compasses 153

Concorde 148
condensation 136
conduction 140, 141
contact lenses 117
continents 30–31
convection 141
core 9
corona 9
craters 10
Cretaceous period 99
crickets 54
crocodiles 60
cylinders 135

D

dandelions 26, 76
day and night 42–43
deafness 120
decay 129
dentine 128
dentists 129
deserts 31, 38–39, 79
digestion 92, 130
dinosaurs 82–100
doctors 109, 113, 125, 133
dormice 57

E

eagles 41
ears 58, 120
Earth 14, 18–19
   crust 20
   day and night 42–43
   evolution 96–97
   gravity 156
   magnetism 153
   plates 20, 22
   rocks 133
earthquakes 20, 49
eclipses 9

eels 64
eggs 57, 61, 63, 64, 68,112–113, 114
Eiffel Tower 135
elbows 109
electricity 16, 29, 138,145, 150–151
elephants 19, 36
emus 37
enamel 128
energy 130, 138–141, 139
Equator 42, 44, 45
eras 97, 98–99
Europe 31
evolution 96–97
exercise 107, 122
experiments 133
extinction 80, 82, 97
eyes 63, 65, 67, 116–117

F

face 107
feet 102
femur 108
fibula 108
fingerprints 105
fins 65
fire 80
fish 50–51, 54, 55,64–65, 97
flies 66
floating and sinking 142–143
flowers 22, 33, 72–73, 80
food 130, 138
forces 154–156
forests 34–35, 40–41,79, 80
fossils 82, 90–91
foxes 35, 38, 55
fractures 109
freckles 104
frogs and toads 40, 54, 62–63
fruit 74–75
fuel 139

G

galaxies 6, 7, 12–13

gases 26, 136–137, 148
gazelles 37
geckos 61
geese 59
genes 112, 113
geologists 133
germination 76–77
germs 105, 125
gibbons 41
gills 64, 65
giraffes 36, 37, 54
glaciers 24, 32
glass 134, 144, 147
glasses 117
gliders 26
goats 23
gods 9, 15, 19
grasshoppers 66
grasslands 36–37
gravity 156
grazes 105
guide dogs 117
gullet 130
gums 128

H

hair 56, 102, 104, 106
head 102, 103, 110
hearing 120
heart 110, 111, 124, 125
heat 140–141
herbivores 56, 92, 94
hibernation 57, 60
hipbones 83, 86, 108
human beings 55, 56, 96,102–130
humerus 108
hummingbirds 41, 58
hurricanes 26, 28

I

ice 33, 136, 137
ice ages 98
incisors 128
inhale 122
insects 66–68, 72

intestines 110, 111, 130
invertebrates 54, 55

J

jawbones 83, 108, 128
jays 35
jellyfish 51
jerboa 39
joints 108, 109
Jupiter 14, 15
Jurassic period 99

K

kangaroos 37
Keller, Helen 120
keratin 106
kidneys 110, 111
knees 108, 109
kookaburras 35

L

lava 20, 21, 137
legs 102, 103
lens 116
light 144–147
lightning 28, 29, 149
limbs 102
lions 36
liquids 136–137, 148, 149
liver 110, 111
lizards 60, 87, 140
loris 41
lungs 110, 111, 122, 124

M

macaws 41
magnets 152–153
mammals 55, 56–57, 98
marine biologists 133
Mars 14, 15
materials 134–137, 144,152
melanin 104
memory 127
Mercury 14, 15
Mesozoic Era 97, 98–99
metamorphosis 66, 68

meteorites 99
mice 54, 57
microscopes 51, 55, 132
midwives 113, 115
milk 56, 137, 139
Milky Way 12–13
mirrors 147
molars 128
moles (skin) 104
monkeys 41
Moon 10–11, 43, 147, 156
moons 15
moose 34
mountains 22–23, 30, 31
muscles 107, 116

N

nails 106
navel 115
neck 103
nectar 72
Neptune 15
nerves 116, 117, 118, 120,
     121, 126–127
newts 62
Niagara Falls 30
North Pole 32, 42, 153
north pole (magnets)
     152–153
nose 108, 118
nuts 75

O

observation 132, 133
oceans 46–47
ocelots 41
oil 139, 145
opaque 144, 145
opticians 117
orbit 9
organs (body) 110–111
ostriches 58, 59
ovaries 112
ovules 74
oxygen 64, 114, 122, 124

P

palaeontologists 82
pancreas 110, 111
pandas 55
parachutes 26, 27
pendulums 154, 155
penguins 30, 32
penis 112
petrol 138, 139
photosphere 8
pigeons 59
pinch marks 105
pine cones 34, 73
pips 74
planets 6, 14–15, 19
plankton 46, 47, 51
plants 51, 70–80, 93, 97,139
plasma 125
platelets 125
platypus 57
Pluto 14, 15
poles 32, 42, 152, 153
pollen 72, 73, 74
pollination 72–73
power stations 150, 151
predators 50
preening 58
prey 50, 58
pterosaurs 98
pulp 128
pumpkins 74
pupils 116, 117
pushing and pulling 154–155

R

rabbits 56–57
racoons 34
radiation 140
radius 108
rain 24, 25
rainbows 144, 145
rainforests 40–41, 79
reflections 147
reflex actions 127
reptiles 55, 60–61, 84, 96,
     98, 140

retinas 116, 117
ribs 83, 108
rivers 24, 30, 31
roadrunners 39
rose hips 74

S

salamanders 62
Saturn 14, 15
scabs 125
scales 60, 65, 86
scanning machines 113
science 132–133
scorpions 38
sea 46–52
sea anemones 51
seals 32
seasons 44–45, 78–79
seeds 26, 38, 72, 74–77, 78
seeing 116–117
senses 116–121, 117, 132
shadows 146
shoulder blades 108
shoulders 109
skeletons 82–83, 100,
     108–109
skin 61, 86, 104–106,121,
     125
skua 33
skulls 83, 88, 92, 108
smelling 118, 119
snakes 41, 60, 61, 87
solar panels 16
Solar System 14–15, 15
solids 136–137, 148, 149
sound 120, 121, 148–149
South Pole 32, 42
south pole (magnets)
     152–153
space stations 16
spacecraft 16, 156
sperm 112, 114
spider webs 135
spinal cord 127
spine 108, 109
spring 44, 78

stamens 72, 73
stars 6–7, 8, 12–13
static electricity 150, 151
steam 136
stethoscopes 125
stomach 110, 111, 130
storms 28–29, 48
structures 134–135
summer 44, 78
Sun 6, 8–9, 14–15, 42–43
sunlight 16, 139, 144–145
swallows 54
swans 58

T
tadpoles 62, 63
tails 64, 82, 94, 95
tapirs 41
tasting 118, 119
teeth 83, 92, 93, 128–129
termites 36
testicles 112
thorax 66
thunder 28, 29, 149
tibia 108
tides 48–49
tongue 119
tornadoes 26, 28

torso 102, 103, 110
tortoises 54, 60, 61
toucans 40
touching 121
translucent 144, 145
transparent 144, 145
trees 34–35, 40–41, 80
triangles 135
Triassic period 98
tsunamis 49
turtles 60, 61
twins 113

U
ulna 108
umbilical cord 114, 115
Universe 6–7
Uranus 14, 15
urine 111

V
vagina 112
valleys 24, 30
veins 70, 71, 124
Venus 14, 15
vertebrates 54, 55
vibrations 120, 148, 149
volcanoes 19, 20–21, 49

W
water 24–25, 70, 71,
   136,142–143
waves
   light 144, 146–147
   sea 48–49
   sound 148–149
wax 136, 137, 145
weather 26–30
weight 156
whales 47, 51, 56, 149
whiskers 57
wind 26–27, 138
windpipe 122
wings 58, 66, 68
winter 44, 78
womb 112, 113, 114–115
woodpeckers 35

X
X-rays 109

Z
zebras 36, 55

Acknowledgments

The publishers would like to thank the following artists for their contribution to this book:
Hemesh Alles (Maggie Mundy Agency Ltd.); Jonathan Adams; Marion Appleton; Mike Atkinson (Garden Studio Illustrators Agents); Craig Austin; Graham Austin; Janet Baker; Julian Baker; Bob Bampton; Julie Banyard; John Barber; Shirley Barker (Artist Partners Ltd.); Denise Bazin; Tim Beer (Maggie Mundy Agency Ltd.); Pierre Bon; Maggie Brand; Derek Brazell; Brighton Illustration Agency; Peter Bull Art Studios; John Butler; Vanessa Card; Diana Catchpole (Linda Rogers Associates); Jonathan Cate; David Cook (Linden Artists); Bob Corley (Artist Partners Ltd.); Joanne Cowne; Jim Channell; Caroline Jane Church; Peter Dennis (Linda Rogers Associates); Kay Dixey; Maggie Downer; Richard Draper; Bernard Duhem; Jean-Philippe Dupong; David Eddington (Maggie Mundy Agency Ltd.); Luc Favreau; Diane Fawcett; Catherine Fichaux; Michael Fisher; Roy Flooks; Chris Forsey; Rosamund Fowler (Artist Partners Ltd.); Andrew French; Tony Gibbons; Mick Gillah; Peter Goodfellow; Matthew Gore; Ray Grinaway; Terry Hadler; Rebecca Hardy; Nick Hawken; Tim Hayward; Ron Haywood; Pierre Hezard; Kay Hodges; Stephen Holmes; Mark Iley; Ian Jackson; John James; Rhian Nest James (Maggie Mundy Agency Ltd.); Ron Jobson; Kevin Jones Associates; David Kearney; Pete Kelly; Roger Kent (Garden Studio Illustrators Agents); Tony Kenyon; Kevin Kimber (B.L. Kearley Ltd.); Deborah Kindred; Stuart Lafford (Linden Artists); Marc Lagarde; Terence Lambert; Stephen Lings (Linden Artists); Bernard Long (Temple Rogers Artists Agents); John Lupton (Linden Artists); Gilbert Macé; Kevin Maddison; Alan Male (Linden Artists); Shirley Mallinson; Maltings Partnership; Josephine Martin (Garden Studio Illustrators Agents); Barry Mitchell; Robert Morton; Patrick Mulrey; David McAllister; Dee McClean (Linden Artists); Polly Noakes (Linda Rogers Associates); Steve Noon (Garden Studio Illustrators Agents); Oxford Illustrators; Darren Pattenden (Garden Studio Illustrators Agents); Jean-Marc Pau; Bruce Pearson; Jane Pickering (Linden Artists); Stephen Player; Sebastian Quigley (Linden Artists); Bernard Robinson; Eric Robson; Michael Roffe; Michelle Ross (Linden Artists); Eric Rowe (Linden Artists); Susan Rowe (Garden Studio Illustrators Agents); Martin Salisbury; Danièle Schulthess; Stephen Seymour; Brian Smith; Guy Smith (Mainline Design); Lesley Smith (John Martin and Artists); Étienne Souppart; John Spires; Clive Spong (Linden Artists); Valérie Stetton; Roger Stewart (Kevin Jones Associates); Tess Stone; Swanston Graphics; Eva Styner; Treve Tamblin (John Martin and Artists); Jean Torton; Shirley Tourret (B.L. Kearley Ltd.); Simon Tegg; Guy Troughton; Michèle Trumel; Visage Design; Vincent Wakeley; Ross Watton (Garden Studio Illustrators Agents); Phil Weare (Linden Artists); Graham White; Joanna Williams; Ann Winterbotham; David Wright

The publishers wish to thank the following for supplying photographs for this book:
Page 82 Ronald Grant Archive; 102 Ronald Grant Archive/DC Comics; 106 Mary Evans Picture Library; 111 Ronald Grant Archive

Thanks also to photographer David Rudkin and models Felicity Lea and Kane Tunmore of Scallywags, and to the World Conservation Monitoring Centre for their kind help